A PHOTOGRAPHIC
HISTORY

A PHOTOGRAPHIC
HISTORY

From the Victorians to the Present Day

Nick Yapp

ARCTURUS

©2003 Getty Images
21-31 Woodfield Road, W9 2BA
email charles.merullo@gettyimages.com

This edition published by Arcturus Publishing Limited, 26-27 Bickles Yard,
151-153 Bermondsey Street, London SE1 3HA, in association with W. Foulsham.

Text ©2003 Nick Yapp

For Getty Images:
Art director: Michael Rand
Design: Tea McAleer
Picture research: Ali Khoja
Editor: Chris Westhorp
Production: Mary Osborne
Proofreader: Liz Ihre
Special thanks: Sam Merullo, Zoltan Mayersberg, Jim Nye and Alexia Shaw

Originated by Imago
Printed and bound by Nuovo Istituto Italiano d'Arti Grafiche, Bergamo, Italy

ISBN 0-572-02942-X (h/b)

ISBN 0-572-02945-4 (p/b)

M 10 9 8 7 6 5 4 3 2 1

(Front Cover) A milkman's rounds uninterrupted
by the Blitz. Fred Morley, October 1940.
(Back Cover) Afghan women shelter from the
wind. Natalie Behring, 27 June 2002.

Introduction

It is doubtful that any century has been so thoroughly, so painstakingly and so graphically recorded as that which began in tumult with the relief of Ladysmith and the first performance of Puccini's Tosca, and ended with the firework displays held around the world to usher in the third Christian millennium. The bulk of what happened in the decades between has been chronicled, photographed, filmed, broadcast, reported and analysed until there is information almost beyond comprehension. We know nearly all we need to know about the 20th century – though there are undoubtedly secrets still to be revealed. What we should now do is apply the lessons the century appears to have tried to teach us.

It was probably the noisiest century ever. Motorised transport replaced horses and carts. The balloon gave way to powered flight, which was then developed into jet aircraft and finally space rockets, which have given us our first footstep into what appears to be the infinity of the universe. On the human scale, where once the loudest entertainment had been marching bands and a singer's lung capacity, amplifiers and loudspeakers brought music thumping through the walls, roofs and ceilings of the world.

Of noise on an Armageddon-like scale, no humble cannon's roar ever matched the crack of an atomic explosion and its potential for doomsday – for the 20th century was also the most destructive century of all time. It has been estimated that more lives were lost in war during those 100 years than in the 1,000 years that preceded them. Incalculable millions died in two world wars, and to this appalling number must be added those slaughtered in civil wars, revolutions (failed and successful) and countless inter-communal outbreaks of violence. To be bricks and mortar was not to be rendered any safer. The buildings of long-established communities were inundated to provide reservoirs. Ancient streets were bulldozed to make way for modern roads and motorways. Mills and factories were demolished to become the graveyard rubble of outmoded industries. Nature suffered too: rainforests were destroyed as loggers bit deeper with their saws and greedy ranchers demanded more grazing land for their beef herds.

Despite all its horrors, the century was also one of amazing hope. The old killers of typhus, cholera, dysentery, malaria, smallpox, scarlet fever, diphtheria and polio were steadily eradicated from much of the planet. People lived longer and healthier lives. In a number of countries, obesity was more of a risk than under-nourishment. Relatively fewer people than in times gone by spent days and nights racked with pain. Although medical care was still only widely available in the developed world, most people believed that all should receive it. The notion that people had a right to be taken care of by the state gradually gained acceptance. New phrases of comfort and reassurance entered the political vocabulary – 'social security', 'old age pensions' and 'national health', though it was never safe to take such measures for granted, and the older the century became, the more at risk they seemed to be.

Above all, it was a century of technological wonder, and the nexus was electricity. It crackled around the world, providing both lighting and heating, but also enabling pumping, lifting, driving, cooking and washing, as well as the enchantment of moving-image entertainment – and advertising. The man who complained towards the end of the 19th century that there was nothing left to invent, was proved wrong a million times over. The 20th century saw the introduction of X-ray machines, microwave ovens, plastics, insulin and penicillin, helicopters and jumbo jets, television and laser surgery, organ transplants and pacemakers, microchips and computers, e-mails and mobile phones, the synchromesh gearbox, skyscrapers and reinforced concrete, battery farming and genetically modified foods, solar power, stereo-recorded sound and cinema, digital cameras and much more. It was only in the second half of the century that some of the delight in the products which electricity had enabled to be created was dimmed by worries about how power was produced – with the potentially high environmental price to be paid by using fossil fuels and atomic energy.

The old dynasties of the Habsburgs, Hohenzollerns and Romanovs, and the empires of the Ottomans and the British, had disappeared – victims of nationalism, democracy and their own incompetence. Out of their ruins came new nation states and leaders, both good and bad: Gandhi, Verwoerd, Mandela, Amin, Hitler, Stalin, Bhutto, Bokassa, Zia, Kenyatta... A new multinational entity appeared – the global corporation. Economic advisers replaced colonial administrators; sales reps replaced colonising armies; and men in suits replaced men in arms. Before the century was out, the flags of Siemens, Exxon, Sony and their like flew from company mastheads in every continent. The logos of Coca-Cola and Microsoft, Shell and McDonalds were recognised everywhere. The desire of the likes of the Disney Corporation to capture the hearts and minds of its targeted masses was reminiscent of the quest for converts that had once been conducted with such zeal by Christian missionaries.

The 20th century was the first to witness non-imperial experiments with world government and global organisations. The League of Nations had arisen out of the carnage of the First World War, fluttered awhile, made a few enemies and then fallen into neglect. Its successor was the United

Nations, in the wake of which came a host of other bodies such as UNESCO, UNRA, WHO, UNICEF, the World Bank and the World Trade Organisation. From outer space came beautifully wondrous, as well as alarming, pictures that showed how tiny and vulnerable our planet appeared and how much it was in need of integrated care, which led to renewed calls and campaigns to protect it.

While all this was going on, the arts seemed to swerve drunkenly from the moderate mainstream into chasms of change. Debussy and Schoenberg took the first steps along a musical path that led, via Stravinsky, Bartok and Shostakovich, to Cage, Boulez and Lutoslawski. The parlour ballad and the music-hall serenade passed through the pens of Kern, Porter and Gershwin, which added sophistication, to become all manner of hits in the 1990s. Post-Impressionism led to 'Op Art' and the 'Dictatorship of the Concept'. The Ballets Russes tiptoed offstage, making way for Tharp, Clark and Cunningham. It was said repeatedly that the modern novel was dead – but it wouldn't lie down. New art forms were born: the musical, the 'sit-com', the documentary, the 'soap', the 'rave', the 'happening'…

What remained at the end of this astonishing century was humankind – it was wounded, frightened, apprehensive, but the species was still very much alive. There was much to fear – AIDS, global warming, terrorism, unprecedented levels of debt, the spectre of chemical and biological war-fare, and those old horsemen of the apocalypse – famine and drought. But there humans were, still trying to improve life by seeking new cures for old diseases, by building new homes, by believing in education, by hoping for peace rather than war and by playing with their children – and still confi-dent that the species would survive another 100 years, or even more…

(previous page) Crowds arrive at Henley Station for the regatta, 4 June 1905.
(above) A trenchful of armed Boer men besieging Mafeking in 1899; the stud-
ied poses – with heads above the parapet and pointed finger – suggest that
this is a publicity photograph set up by Reinhold Thiele. (opposite) Soldiers of
the Royal Canadian Regiment attacking a hill near Sunnyside farm, 1900.

*When the Second South African War, or Boer War, began in 1899,
the British and the Dutch settlers (known as Boers) had already
been at odds in the continent for a century. But when acrimony
turned to war it was an ill-matched contest – yet one that the
British almost lost within a single 'Black Week'. In the end, might
overcame cunning and the Boers finally capitulated in 1902.*

(clockwise, from the top) A British field hospital in the Boer War; wounded Afrikaners at Wijnberg Hospital, Pretoria; and a blindfolded German intermediary is brought in to camp by British troops to negotiate a surrender.

(opposite) A Regent Street flower-seller, old enough to be Eliza Doolittle's mother, prepares roses for her customers, London 1900. (top) A cat-and-dog-meat man caters for his own regulars. (above) A break from picking strawberries and time for a drink and a cigarette.

Very different strata of Edwardian society. (top) Vagrants asleep in St James's Park, London, October 1900. (above) Wash night in a well-kept slum tenement where things are tidy and respectable.

(top) Well-shod members of the Ranelagh Golf Club, London, take tea in the clubhouse. (above) Gentlemen begin their after-supper smoke, with the pipe proving particularly popular with the satisfied diners.

'Be it never so humble...' (clockwise, from the top) The female members of a middle-class family; a maid prepares breakfast for her master and mistress; and an Edwardian family takes tea in the back parlour.

Two panoramas by A.H. Robinson, c.1910. (top) The regatta at Cowes, Isle of Wight. (above) A real castle on the shore, a fleeting one in the sand... Bamburgh stands guard over a Northumbrian beach.

Hot air and warm breezes... On a beautiful day in May 1909, contestants and their followers prepare for a hot air balloon race at the Hurlingham Club, a fashionable sporting venue in West London where such rallies took place regularly.

For the truly intrepid pioneer traveller there was only one direction in the 1900s – and that was upwards. The work of the Wright brothers, using gliders and experimental, powered machines, had inspired many others to take to the air. Such public interest only aided the popularity of the relatively old-fashioned balloon.

(top) One small gudgeon attracts the attention of schoolboy anglers, London 1905. (above) Boys dressing after a late swim in Hyde Park's Serpentine, October 1900.

(top) A cunning contrivance to aid a swimming lesson in the River Thames at Wallingford, September 1906.
(above) Boys at Westminster School fight for crumbs during the Pancake Greaze on Shrove Tuesday, 1905.

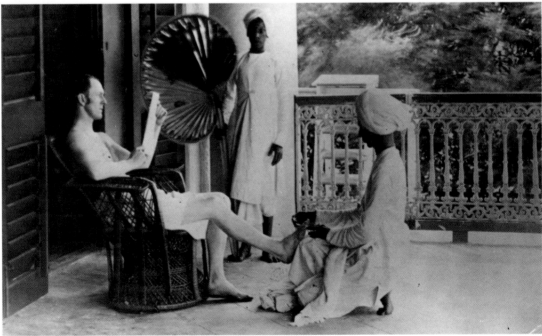

Away from home... (top) 'If you want to know the way, ask a policeman...' An old lady in London, 1910. (above) An Englishman abroad reads the news from home on the verandah of his bungalow, India 1900.

(top) Ladies take tea during an outing to Loughton, Essex, August 1908. (above) Unionist whip Lord Valentia entertains Indian military representatives to the coronation of King Edward VII, 1902.

Dressed to impress. (clockwise, from top left) Tweed in the nursery, *c.*1900. Miss Kennedy Stott, 6 May 1904. Camille Clifford. Master Trotter, April 1902. The Neaver de Montes in school uniform, May 1902.

(opposite) The Italian airship *Parseval* passes the Campanile of San Marco, Venice. (above) the Comte Charles de Lambert pilots his *Wright Flyer* over Paris, 18 October 1909.

(previous page) The first powered, sustained and controlled flight by a heavier-than-air machine. While Wilbur Wright runs alongside, his brother Orville takes off from the sands at Kill Devil Hills, Kitty Hawk, North Carolina, on 17 December 1903. Flyer I was powered by a 25-horsepower engine which enabled the plane to stay aloft for just under a minute and cover some 852 feet.

(above) Would-be immigrants from Europe bound for New York crammed on board the Red Star liner *Westernland,* 1901 (right). New arrivals are inspected on Ellis Island for signs of disease, which if found resulted in them being sent back to Europe, *c.*1900.

They came in their millions – the Old World's poor, the wretched, the huddled masses. As many as 8,000 immigrants to the New World were processed on Ellis Island in New York harbour every day, where they were inspected, tested, often renamed, and sent on their way if accepted. The procedure was described by one immigrant as 'din, confusion, bewilderment, madness!', but it served to populate a vast land in need of labour.

Ellis Island, 1905. (clockwise, from the top) An immigration official labels a German family; a mother and her children wait in the baggage hall; Jakob Muthelstadt and family, en route to North Dakota.

(previous page) The aftermath of the San Francisco earthquake, 1906.
(above, clockwise from top left) Jean Jaurès, French socialist leader (third
from left). A hatless Ramsay MacDonald. David Lloyd George in his garden.
Winston Churchill. (opposite) The young Mohandas Karamchand Gandhi.

*'Bliss was it in that dawn to be alive', and to be a young politician
was very heaven. Middle class liberals and socialists competed to
improve the condition of humanity. It was an age of such innova-
tions as old age pensions, National Insurance, death duties on rich
estates, and constitutional reform. And, for some, it was a time
when great empires were called into question.*

Members of the court of Tsar Nicholas II, Russia's last monarch, attending a family picnic, *c.*1910. A court member is playing with one of the Tsar's daughters in the foreground.

The decade leading up to the First World War was the swansong of a number of Europe's monarchies. Many kings were yet to be adequately constrained by more democratic, constitutional measures to prevent them interfering in the political process. In Russia, autocracy rather than democracy was the tsar's instinct and revolution simmered.

Constructing the socialist order... Vladimir Ilyich Ulyanov, better known as Lenin, at work some years before the Bolshevik Revolution.

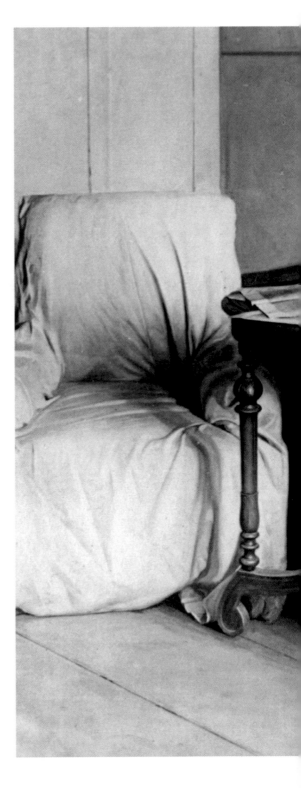

Perhaps more than any other politician, Lenin shaped the 20th century. His adult life was dedicated to establishing Marxist rule. He was the shrewd architect of the Bolshevik Revolution in Russia, which transformed the political landscape in Europe and beyond.

It was an intensely exciting and creative artistic age. In painting, Impressionism had given way to a variety of fresh genres. In music, a number of large new concert halls provided magnificent venues for masterpieces by Ravel and Debussy, Elgar and Mahler, Stravinsky and Schoenberg. The opera houses were filled by audiences eager to hear works by Puccini, Richard Strauss and Wolf-Ferrari. Theatre-goers were thrilled to watch plays by Wilde, Shaw, Chekhov, Synge, Galsworthy and Hauptmann. The shelves of bookshops and libraries held the latest works by Mann, Wells, Forster, Wharton, James and Zola. And, across the Atlantic, jazz musician Buddy Bolden was just warming up...

(top) Samuel Langhorne Clemens, better known as Mark Twain. (above) Auguste Rodin in his museum at Meudon. (opposite) Leo Tolstoy, with his wife Sonya, 1906.

The conquest of the American West was turned into theatrical entertainment starring some of its real-life participants. (above) William F. Cody, better known as Buffalo Bill, originator of Buffalo Bill's Wild West Show. (opposite) One of the show's star attractions was Phoebe Moses, better known as sharpshooter Annie Oakley, 'Little Sure Shot', who could hit the thin edge of a playing card from 30 paces.

(previous page) Ballet rehearsals at the Metropolitan Opera House, New York, 1900. The fleshy delights of Paris during *la belle epoque*. (above) A tableau of 'devilish delights' at the music hall of La Cirque, 1900. (opposite) Joy on the wing at the Folies-Bergère, *c*.1910.

Martyrs to fashion. (above) The French actress Gaby Deslys poses for Henry Guttman, c.1910. (opposite) A dancer at the Folies-Bergère, 1905, though presumably not in her stage outfit.

Wonder of the age – the 'horseless carriage'. (top) C.S. Rolls takes the future King George V for a spin. (opposite) A motorcab overtakes a horse-drawn hansom. (above) Henry Ford outside his Detroit factory.

Just a few of the new electric 'toys' that delighted many in the 1900s... (clockwise, from above) An electric bath, the forerunner of the sunbed, at the Light Care Institute. A British Army hearing test, c.1905. The automatic boot-polishing machine, November 1907. Measuring brain activity with a Lavery Electric Phrenometer, August 1907.

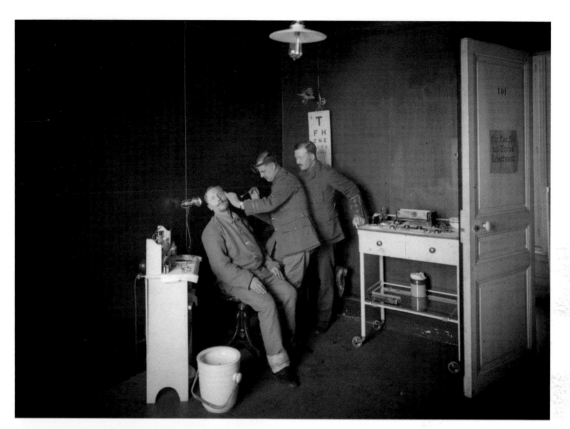

Like a child delighted with a new toy, the world was fascinated by electricity. By 1900 there were 250 suppliers of the magic force in Britain and 3000 in America. The largest generator was German – a 1500 kilowatt machine at Elberfeld. But supply was chaotic. The battle between AC and DC still raged, and there was to be no standardisation of voltage supply for decades.

Food for rich palates. (top) Forcing early vegetables under cloches, 1908. (above) The kitchens of the Hotel Cecil in London's Strand. Frequented by the rich, the Cecil was the largest hotel in Europe.

(top) Bottles of champagne in one of the Roman cellars of a chateau at Reims. (above) The packing department of a small factory bottling fruit – an expensive delicacy aimed at the well-to-do.

Increasingly, work on the land was available only to the specialist labourer.
(above) Bronco-busting at Matador Ranch, Texas, 1908. (opposite) Itinerant
shearers at work on a sheep farm in Westmoreland, the Lake District.

*The rhythms of English rural life remained largely intact: teams of
oxen could still be seen ploughing; village schools were closed during haymaking time; animal dung had yet to be replaced by artifi-
cial fertilisers; and there was still work for the mole-catcher, the
woodcutter and the pedlar. But the old ways were under threat,
and few of them survived beyond 1914.*

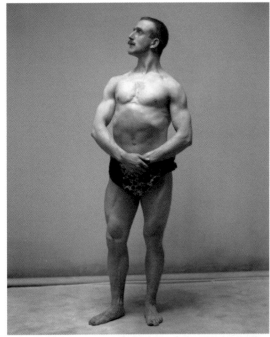

The male body beautiful. (clockwise, from top left) Frederick Grace, 1908. Mr Murray, bodybuilder, 1905. Goldsmith and Hewitt, 1908. Alfred Shrubb, 1910. James J. Jeffries, 1900.

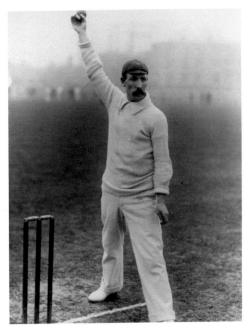

(clockwise, from top left) American Jim Thorpe throws for Olympic gold, Stockholm, 1912. Mr Bryce on the golf links. George Burdett keeping goal for Woolwich Arsenal, 1911. Walter Mead, a rare professional cricketer in the Essex Eleven. Heavyweight boxing champion, Jack Johnson.

(right) A couple take a dip in the briny at Ostend, Belgium, 1911.

Jack Frost exerts his icy grip. (above) The Oxfordshire landscape is transformed to the enjoyment of many, 30 January 1912. (left) A Guards officer and his partner take to the pond ice in a London park, 1919.

The magnificence of manned flight. (top) British aviator Claude Grahame-White takes off from outside the White House, Washington, DC, on 4 October 1910. (above) A modern Bristol Prier monoplane circles ancient Stonehenge, 1911. (opposite) Male fascination: an aviation meeting at Hendon Aerodrome in May 1911, established that year by Claude Grahame-White.

The start of the 100-mile Indianapolis Motor Speedway, 1910. Racing cars had already reached speeds of well over 100mph. The first Indianapolis 500 was run on a newly surfaced track a year later.

(top) The west crossover on the Central London Railway, outside Liverpool Street Station, 30 July 1912. (above) A London & North Western Railway Company (L&NWR) signals gantry at Rugby, 1910. (opposite) Princess Ludwig of Lowenstein-Westheim learns to fly, 12 June 1914.

By the 1910s, the railway boom had passed its peak, though new lines were still being constructed, both above and below ground. The new wonder of the day was air travel, which was thrilling but uncomfortable. When the first scheduled flights began in 1919, passengers were advised to wear heavy coats because of the cold, and to stuff their ears with cotton wool to keep out the noise.

(previous page) Capturing a pre-war golden afternoon with a Kodak camera, 1910. Music and movement. (top) The Gills perform the Brazilian Maxixa, January 1914. (above) A Decca gramophone is used to provide music afloat, August 1919. (opposite) The Beauty Chorus attains shellac immortality, January 1916.

(above) Thomas Alva Edison checks the quality of a gramophone, one of his most famous inventions, 27 October 1911. (opposite) 'Seated one day at the follyphone...' Mr Lewis Sydney with a less likely contender for consumer sales and longevity, September 1912.

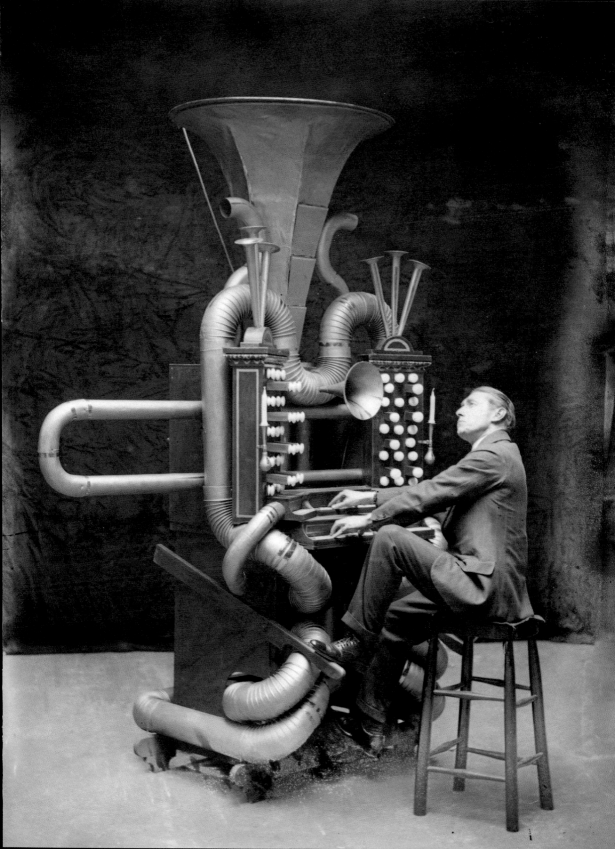

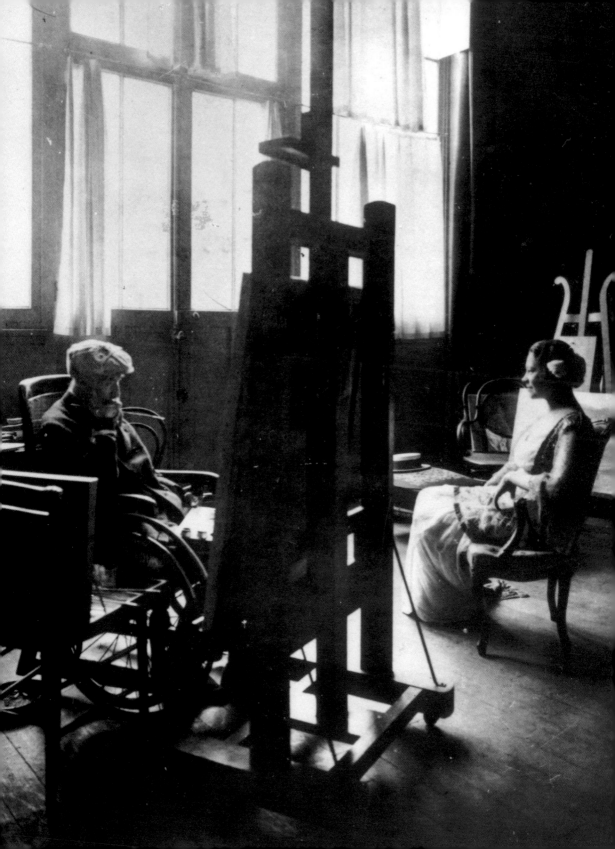

Old masters and young innovators. (clockwise, from opposite) Auguste Renoir in his studio at Les Collettes, Cagnes, France, 1915; Charlie Chaplin behind the camera, 1915; Marcel Proust, *c.*1910; and Henri Matisse in Paris, May 1913.

The spirit of revolution – a desire for innovation, transformation and reinvention – had animated artistic traditions long before it provided the catalyst for the overthrow of the political order. Fauvism and Cubism were just two of the 'isms' of the age. The writings of Proust, Gide, D.H. Lawrence, Joyce and Kafka tested readers. The silent cinema, by contrast, provided its pleasures while making fewer demands of its audience.

In her prime... (above) Anna Pavlova and Laurent Novikov in Glazunov's
Bacchanale, c.1913. (opposite) Mikhail Fokine and Vera Fokina, stars of the
Ballets Russes, in Rimsky-Korsakov's *Scheherezade*, c.1910.

The spirit of the dance took bold new steps. In Russian ballet,
the order and discipline of Petipa was replaced by the exuberance
and expressionism of new dancer-artistes, especially those under
the spell of Diaghilev, founder of Ballets Russes in Paris (1909).
In popular dance it was an era when the tango held sway and the
Astaires hit the Broadway boards. But the most famous single step
of all was Nijinsky's leap in La Spectre de la Rose.

Exceptional people... (clockwise, from opposite top) Sixteen-year-old Marisana is seven feet, four inches tall while eighteen-year-old Asia is just two feet, two inches; London Olympia, 1914. Giant Machnow and Madam Chiquita, *c.*1910. A German couple with a combined weight of 1,032lbs. A circus wedding, Stepney, East London, 1913.

GIANT MACHNOW & M[...] CH[...]

Home Secretary Winston Churchill (with top hat and without an umbrella visible) visiting the scene of the anarchist siege in Sidney Street, Stepney, London, 3 January 1911.

(clockwise, from above) Police officers restrain a Suffragette outside Buckingham Palace on 21 May 1914. At the same palace protest, Emmeline Pankhurst is removed by Superintendent Rolfe. A 'bright young thing' studies a Suffragette pamphlet. The joint founders of the movement, Emmeline Pankhurst and her daughter Christabel (left and right respectively), in prison uniform, October 1908.

A martyr to the Suffragette cause – Emily Davison throws herself under the King's horse Anmer during the Epsom Derby, 4 June 1913.

The movement was founded by Emmeline Pankhurst in 1889. Over the next 25 years, the Suffragettes, as those seeking votes for women were called, conducted a determined, violent and much derided campaign to get Votes for Women. They endured imprisonment, forced feeding, public humiliation – and death in some cases – for a cause that struck at the very heart of sexual discrimination.

(top) Taking the plunge and cooling off in the waters of the Serpentine Lido in London's Hyde Park, 1911. (above) The ladies football team from Harrods, the Knightsbridge store, line up at Barnes, 1917.

(top) Parading for the camera... More recruits parading for the sergeant... same day, same duty room.
(above) Taking the oath... new female recruits to the police force, 30 January, 1917.

A surfeit of war. (top) A supporter of Sun Yat Sen is executed by rival Chinese soldiers, 1912. (above) Dead on the battlefield of Adrianople during the Balkan Wars, October 1913.

(top) Controlling the Khyber Pass, Afghanistan, against all-comers – local warriors, *c*.1910.
(above) The Grand Plaza, Mexico City, during American intervention in the civil war, 1914.

(above) Nedeljko Cabrinovic is arrested following a failed assassination attempt against Archduke Franz Ferdinand on 28 June 1914. However, not long afterwards, one of his accomplices, Gavrilo Princip, succeeded and killed both the archduke and his consort, Sophie, Duchess von Hohenberg. (opposite) The late archduke's blood-spattered tunic.

It was a murderous act that was described as 'the spark that set the world ablaze': a group of six Serbian nationalist extremists had gathered in Sarajevo to kill the heir apparent to the Austro-Hungarian Empire – and they had triumphed. In the weeks that followed the archduke's death, ultimatums flew from one European power to another, and with grotesque speed and almost unstoppable momentum much of the continent soon found itself at war.

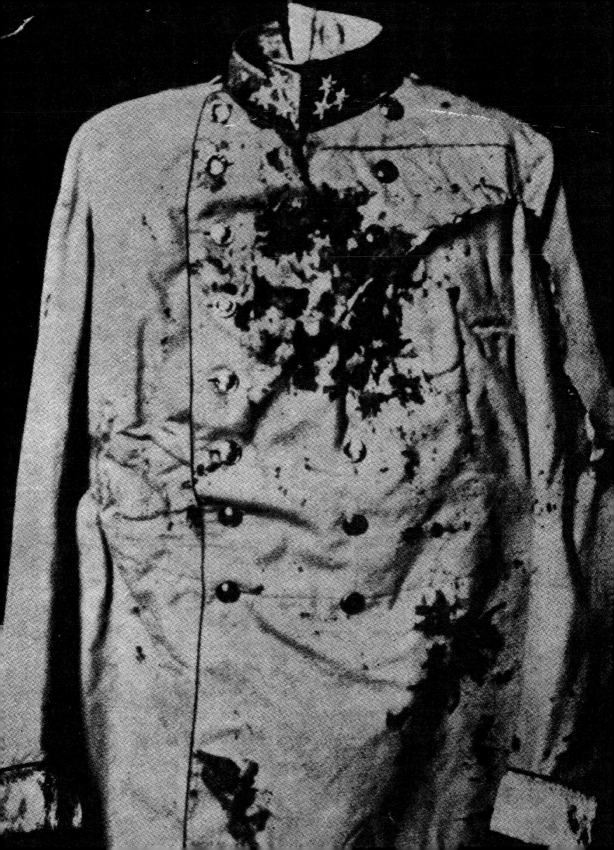

(above) A British 'Tommy' and his loved one part at Victoria Station, December 1914. (left) German troops leave for the front, 1914. (opposite) A 'Doughboy' from New York goes off to participate in the war in Europe, 1917. (following page) No Man's Land, Gondrecourt, 15 August 1918. But these terrifying scenes were yet to come; at the outset it was time for loving farewells.

The killing began on 4 August 1914. When it stopped in November 1918, it had cost the lives of more than 5,000 men a day. No one had expected such carnage; it had been said that it will be 'all over by Christmas'. As if they were setting out on a summer excursion, young men had chalked 'TO PARIS' or 'TO BERLIN' on the carriages that were whisking them to their deaths.

(clockwise, from the top) A stretcher party in the hellish, shell-churned mud of Passchendaele, 1 August 1917. French *poilu*s fight and die for Verdun, 1917. C Battery, 6th American Field Artillery, at Beaumont, 12 September 1918.

Russian field gunners on the Eastern Front, 1914. The angle of the guns' barrels suggests that the enemy was at alarmingly close quarters.

In Russia, anti-war feeling had been quite pronounced beforehand, but once the hostilities began it was patriotism rather than pacifism that carried the day. Only a few thousand Russians resisted the call to arms over the next three years. Although blessed by the tsar and led into battle by priests, the poorly equipped Russian Army eventually suffered a string of defeats that contributed to revolution.

(clockwise, from above) The last moments of the German battlecruiser *Blücher* at Dogger Bank on 24 January 1915 – nearly 800 crew members drowned. The 'terror of the seas' – a German U-boat surfaces, 1917. The engine room of a U-boat.

New perspectives on warfare were provided by the cine-camera and the fighter plane. A cameraman from the US Army films a Nieuport-28 biplane taking off during the Allied counter-offensive in summer 1918.

Cause and effect... (above) German troops release poison gas in 1915. (right) British soldiers, who have been blinded by mustard gas, stand in line at a dressing station near Béthune, 10 April 1918 – a scene that was immortalised in a painting by the American artist who took the photograph, John Singer Sargent.

The War To End All Wars, as it became known afterwards, earned this sobriquet partly as a result of the industrialisation of mass slaughter – in addition to the horrors of poisoned gas, mortal men had to contend with the witheringly rapid fire of machine guns, massive bombardments of artillery shells, mines, hand grenades, flame-throwers, tanks, and fighter and bomber aircraft. Their protection consisted of holes in the ground, sandbags and tin helmets.

War leaders in waiting. (opposite, right) Corporal Adolf Hitler during his convalescence at a military hospital in Pasewalk, Pomerania, 1914. (above, right) Colonel Winston Churchill with Sir Archibald Sinclair at Armentières, 11 February 1916.

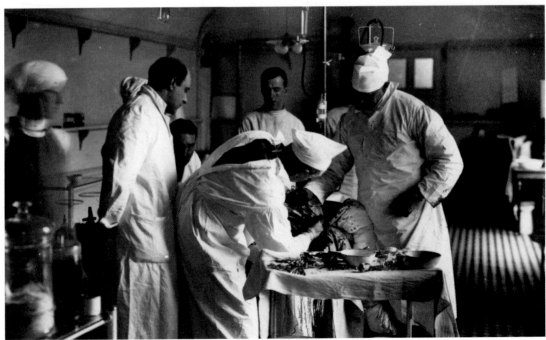

(previous page) An air-raid drill at Hither Green, South London, 1917. (top) Soldiers enjoy a 'kaiser shy' at Sidcup Fair, 1917. (above) An amputation at the Duchess of Westminster Military Hospital, 1915.

(top) Patients with 'shell-shock' undergo experimental medical treatment, 1917. (above) Troops arrive at a concert for the wounded held at the Savoy Hotel, London, in March 1916.

Unrest in Ireland. (clockwise, from the top) Police charge strikers in Dublin, August 1913 – the battle left one man killed and 500 injured. British troops engage Irish Republicans during the Easter Rising, April 1916. Children collect firewood from buildings ruined in the Easter troubles.

War in the East. (left, top) German troops equipped with artillery block rail lines during a battle with irregular soldiers. (left, bottom) Russian troops surrender en masse as their country's war effort collapsed suddenly in 1917.

On the Eastern Front, the end, when it came, was swift. By July 1917, the tsar had abdicated, Kerensky's offensive had ground to a halt in Galicia, revolt had broken out in the Ukraine, and Russian troops had begun to desert in droves. Four months later, the Bolsheviks seized power, declared a ceasefire and opened peace negotiations with Germany at Brest-Litovsk.

Expectation. (above) The crew of HMS *Victory* on parade, 4 October 1918.
Fulfilment. (opposite) Crowds in London celebrate the signing of the Armistice
on 11 November 1918.

When peace eventually came it was greeted with hysterical relief
in London, Paris and New York. Normal life ceased. Crowds ran
wild. People leapt and danced with joy. Strangers copulated in the
street. In Berlin, relief was muted. Broken men, dressed in rags and
with grief in their eyes, staggered back from the trenches, ashamed
at what had happened.

Allied officers peer into the Hall of Mirrors as delegates sign one of the series of separate treaties that made up the Peace of Versailles, 28 June 1919. The foundations of a rickety new Europe were being laid.

The presiding genius at the Versailles negotiations was President Woodrow Wilson of the United States. In broad terms, this was an attempt by the victors to lay out a new future for Europe. However, there were some powerful voices, including Clemenceau of France, who desired that Germany take special responsibility for having caused the war and compensate the sufferers accordingly, which resulted in a costly and contentious bill for reparations.

(clockwise, from the top) Stalin, Lenin and Kalinin at the Congress of the Russian Communist Party in March 1919. Tsar Nicholas II and his family in captivity at Tobolsk, 1918. Members of a female battalion of the Russian Army, 1917.

(top) Delicate balance on display in the women's egg-and-spoon race at the Merton Park Military Sports, August 1918. (above) Captain de Tessier stoops to conquer at the Queen's Club, London.

(top) Miss May Turner in full flow, also at the Queen's Club, London, August 1918. (above) Away from the Field of Mars... it's the men's turn, as a military tug-of-war team digs in its heels at Merton Park.

(previous page) Henry Ford's gift to the workers of the world was the assembly line. By this time, c.1920, the Ford Motor Company was turning out more than 4,000 cars a day – 'in any colour so long as it's black'. (left) A day at the races... Spectators relax during the Whitsun meeting held at the Brooklands racing car circuit, June 1922.

People's quest for pleasure was strong in the 1920s in the wake of the nightmare of the First World War. Young and old, rich and poor, worker and pleasure-seeking 'flapper' alike invested time and energy in parties and pastimes – which could be anything from non-stop dance contests to a day out in the open-top 'flivver'.

A beggar jogs alongside the carriage seeking a small charitable gift from King George V (on the left in the rear seat) and his fellow passengers at the Epsom Derby, June 1920.

As a father and husband, King George V took his role sufficiently seriously that he believed his children should be frightened of him. As a monarch, his interference in politics was infrequent and benign. For a hobby he collected stamps and as a sportsman he liked shooting and tennis.

Rights and duties. (top) A children's march in West London (presumably under Salvation Army orders) in support of Prohibition measures for Britain, June 1917. (opposite) A child worker in a textile factory, 1910.

In the early 20th century children knew their place. They respected their elders, were obedient to authority and, more often than not, did as instructed. Slowly, children were afforded protection from the drudgery of work and the exploitation of employers. Children were being provided with new opportunities through education, and although school meant discipline it also fostered happiness.

Temporary accommodation. (top) Adults and children await a meal at an institute for the poor in Bucharest, *c.*1920. (above) Worcester's former prison becomes housing for the homeless, 1926.

(top) A New York meeting hall is turned into a dormitory, *c.*1928. (above) Boxes in the Opera House in Athens become bedsits during a housing shortage in the city, *c.*1925.

Hands up!... (top) Unemployed workers in Germany hold out their identification papers in a Berlin employment agency, c.1920. (above) A squad of cyclists salute Benito Mussolini in November 1923, when Italy had already become a one-party state.

(top) Some 80,000 political activists take an oath of allegiance to Hitler in the Lustgarten, Berlin, 1925.
(above) The guests offer a fashionably stiff-armed salute as the happy couple cut their wedding cake with an axe at a Woodcraft ceremony in Fordingbridge on 14 April 1928.

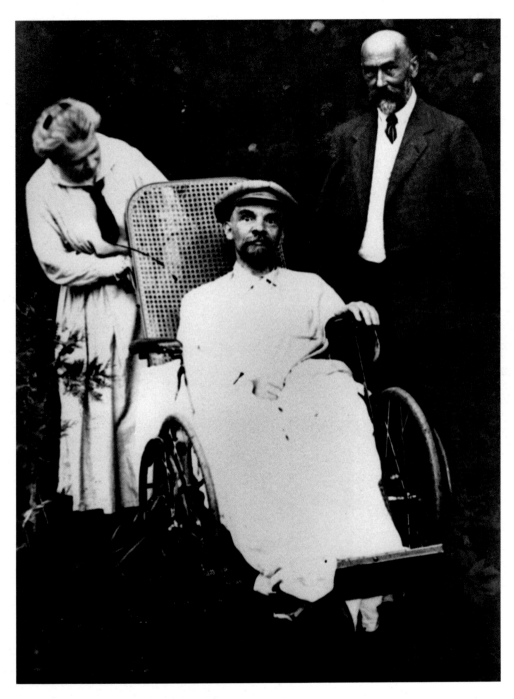

Mentor and successor. (above) An ailing Lenin a few days before his death, his mind shattered by a series of strokes. (opposite) Iosif Dzhugashvili, better known as Stalin (the name he adopted from the word *stal* or "steel"), now manoeuvred himself to become the heir to the Revolution.

Adolf Hitler rehearses the exaggerated, theatrical gestures with which he intends to accompany his speeches, recorded by the camera of Heinrich Hoffmann in 1925.

An era of collective effort and extremist views. (clockwise, from the top) A physical culture parade in Red Square, 1927. The fledgling Communist Party of Great Britain celebrates May Day in 1928. German members of the anti-Nazi *Rotfront* pictured in September 1928.

Many hands make much profit. (top) Flower-packers handle the daffodil harvest at Long Rock, Cornwall, 1926. (above) The production line at a dried fig factory in Smyrna, Turkey, c.1925.

Many women kept their jobs when the men came home... (top) Harvesting maize at Hoddesdon, Hertfordshire, 1927. (above) Icing biscuits at the W. & R. Jacob's factory in Liverpool, 1926.

The magic and misery of water. (top) A family tests the temperature at Clacton, Essex, in June 1922. (above) A couple set out in unwelcoming weather for one of Brighton's piers in 1929.

(top) Horseplay in the shallows at Shanklin, Isle of Wight, 6 August 1928. (above) A London policewoman pursues some would-be bathers unencumbered by costumes in Hyde Park, 1926.

Shaking the blues away... (top) The Alfred Jackson Dancing Girls, June 1928. (above) Percival Mackey, his band, and his wife Monti Ryan on the roof of the London Palladium, 1927. (opposite) Dancing the Charleston at the Shaftesbury Theatre, London, October 1926.

Lost in the languor of a pose... (above) A model wears a 'Palm Beach ensemble', c.1925. (opposite) Joan Crawford models a 'flapper' outfit, c.1929 – one film critic wrote about Crawford that 'her shoulders were more expressive than her face'.

The 'old equaliser'... (opposite) Employees of America's Cleveland Trust Company prepare to defend the main vault, *c.*1924. (top) A police shooting contest at Petersham, England, 1922. (above) A gendarme takes aim during pistol training in Paris, 1929.

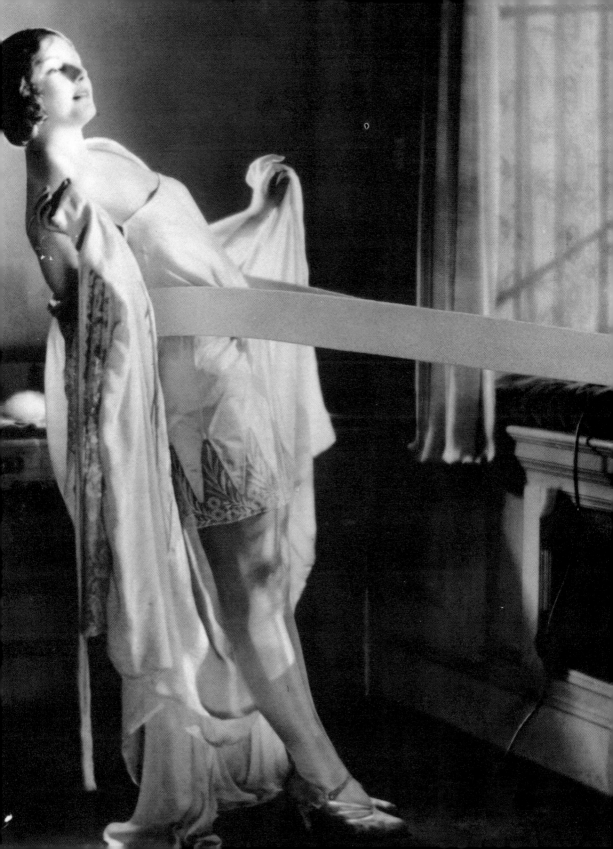

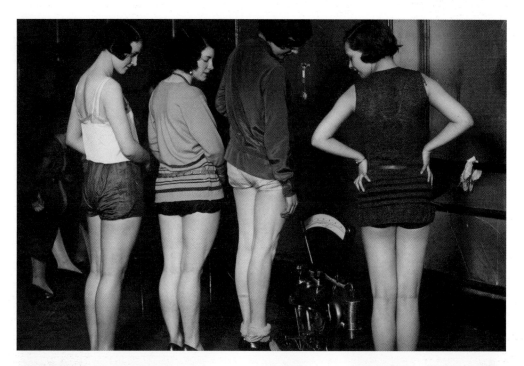

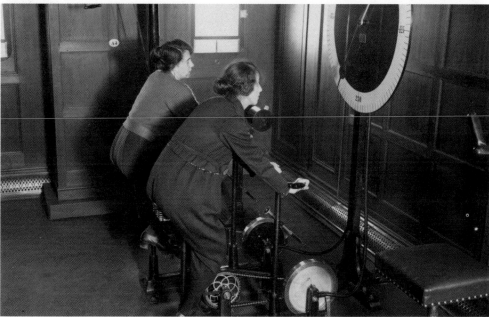

Health and Fitness. (opposite) The Vibro-Slim machine gets to work, *c*.1928. (top) A quartet of C.B. Cochran's Young Ladies, *c*.1925. (above) Whiling away the hours and whittling away the excess inches for passengers in the gym on board the White Star liner *Homeric*, February 1922.

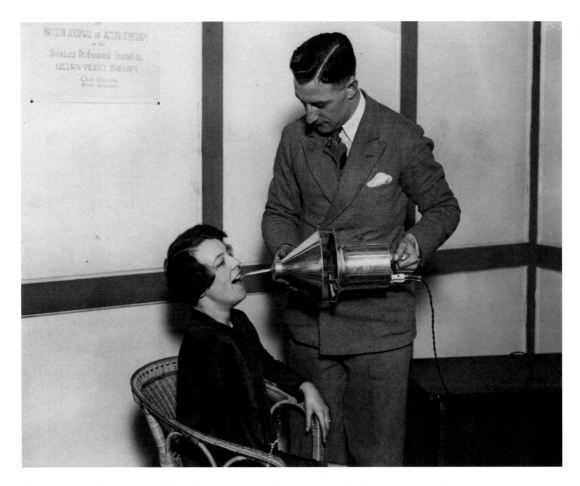

Caring contraptions. (above) The 'Sunviray' dental lamp makes its first
appearance at the International Exhibition of Light and Heat in Medicine, held
in Westminster, December 1927. (opposite) The Metalix Tube for Therapy
being demonstrated at work, November 1928.

*It was a golden age of gadgetry – machines that healed, removed,
destroyed, regenerated, rejuvenated... The only requirements
appeared to be a motor, a supply of electricity, some rubber tubing,
a metal canister, plenty of valves, and an endless supply of people
to experiment upon. Scientists seemed to be capable of almost anything – and they attempted pretty much everything.*

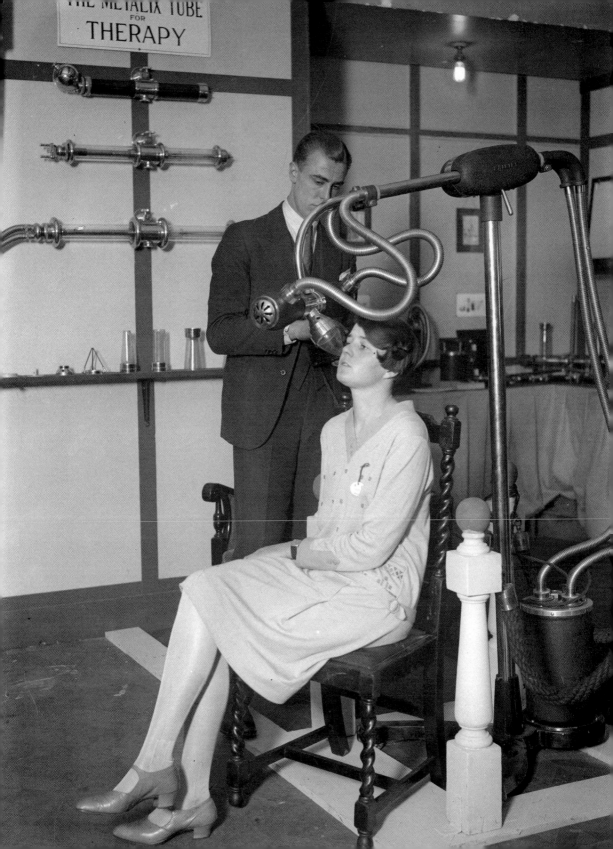

(opposite) The mayor of Henley-on-Thames tees off, October 1927. (top) Lady Champion of the Lyceum Billiards Club, Mrs Eddowes, attempts a swerve shot, 1926. (above) Members of the Arsenal team limber up, 1927 ('Woolwich' was now dropped).

Clowns and puppets. (opposite) Charlie Chaplin with a miniature version of his famous tramp character, the 'little fellow'. (above) Buster Keaton admires a gift from a German woodcarver.

The test and racing track on the roof of the Fiat works in Turin, December 1929. The track and factory were designed by Giacomo Matte-Trucco in 1899 for Giovanni Agnelli, the founder of Fiat.

The great names in motoring during the 1920s were those of the founding fathers of car production – Morris, Ford, Peugeot, Citroën, Ferrari, Daimler, Benz, Chrysler, Austin, Bentley, Rolls and Royce. The Fiat name was an exception – an abbreviation of Fabbrica Italiana di Automobili Torino.

High fliers. (opposite) Testing the aptitude of applicants for the job of painting the Brooklyn Bridge, New York, April 1926. (top) Construction workers in London take a lunch break, April 1929. (above) Repairing the roof of South London's Crystal Palace, June 1927.

Flying could not yet match the style and comfort of rail travel, though meals were served on planes, smoking was allowed, and even the crew enjoyed the occasional cocktail. Modern rail expresses offered dining cars, observation coaches, sleeping cars, Pullman luxury coaches, and some-times even library cars and grand pianos.

Transports of delight. (clockwise, from opposite, top) In-flight service, Paris to London, April 1929. Lufthansa passengers about to enjoy the first ever in-flight movie, April 1925. A third-class sleeper with the LNER (London and North Eastern Railway) company, September 1928. A sleeping compartment on board one of the trains of the US railroad network, September 1928.

Food, fresh or fast... (above) Countless Christmas turkeys hanging at a Watling Street butcher's shop, London, December 1929. (opposite) Catering for the hungry traveller – a trio of chocolate, fruit, snack and sweet vending machines at London's Paddington Station, January 1929.

Most of the food to be had in the 1920s was still fresh rather than frozen, tinned or 'convenience'. Although in general people were better fed than at any time since their families had first left the land for the towns, a significant number of families still faced the prospect of a feast-free Christmas without a goose or turkey.

(previous page) Workers from the refreshment room at London's Paddington Station take a break on the roof of their 'live-in' hostel, August 1935.(above) A short hop... Holidaymakers about to take a 'joy flight' over the island of Jersey, 6 August 1934. (opposite) Long haul... The cast of the New York Midnight Follies alight from Imperial Airways Hannibal-class *Horatius* at Croydon Airport, 5 October 1933.

Women took to the air in large numbers in the 1930s – mostly as passengers, but many as flight crew and a famous few as pilots. There weren't many film stars who were considered more glamorous than Amy Johnson and Amelia Earhart, whose pioneering flights captured the public's attention worldwide. But tragedy struck: Earhart and her plane disappeared over the central Pacific in 1937 and Johnson was never found after baling out of her plane over the Thames estuary in 1941.

(above) A team of Berlin policemen help to moor the *Graf Zeppelin* airship, *c.*1936. (opposite) The giant emerges... Crowds in Tokyo gathered in awe outside the *Graf Zeppelin* hangar, *c.*1930.

Until one fatal day in 1937, airships were the monarchs of the skies. They had proved themselves to be quieter and steadier in flight than any airplane, and they offered a standard of travelling comfort and luxury that only the Atlantic liners could surpass. 'The Graf Zeppelin,*' reported Lady Grace Drummond Hay, 'is more than just machinery, canvas and aluminium. It has a soul.'*

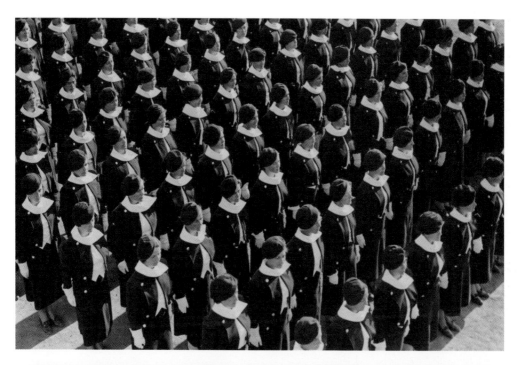

Fascism on parade... (clockwise, from opposite top) Girl members of Giovani Italiane, Italy, c.1930. Adolf Hitler at Bückeberg, October 1934; at Lipski in Poland, March 1935; and in his Nuremberg heartland.

The nightmare begins... (above) Nazi street thugs pose with their victims on the streets of Cuxhaven, 27 July 1933. (opposite) Joseph Goebbels, Nazi head of the National Ministry for Public Enlightenment and Propaganda, c.1935.

Nazi persecution of the Jews began in earnest in 1933. Jewish shops were looted and Jews were forced to scrub the streets, while their goods and property were expropriated. In the photograph above, Oskar Danker and his partner Adele have been forced to wear placards. His reads: 'As a Jew I only take German girls to my room.' Hers reads: 'I'm fit for the greatest swine and only get involved with Jews.' Much worse was to come.

Shed a little happiness... (top) German forest nymphs, *c.*1935. (above) Three members of the chorus line from the Piccadilly Hotel cabaret, *c.*1935. (opposite) C.B. Cochran's Young Ladies (left to right: Sonia Hully, Yvonne Robinson and Bubbly Rogers) at the Palace Theatre, 1934.

(top) A little early in the season... Friends frolic on the banks of the River Arun, West Sussex, 2 April 1938. (above) Clubbing, 1930s-style – an exercise class display their precision in November 1932.

(top) Taking your partner for a spin... Naturists exercise instinctive rights and freedoms, c.1935. (below) Tiller boys... The Cambridge University Boat race team tone up with a touch of Swedish dancing, 16 February 1939.

(opposite) Hiding one's face... A fashion shot of a gant de tulle stockingette and lace glove, 1934. (top) Baring one's back... at Thorpe Bay, Essex, 5 August 1934. (above) Balling the jack... at Stanley Park, Blackpool, 11 June 1938.

(opposite) Kurt Hutton's seminal portrait from November 1939 of one of the 35 per cent unemployed in Wigan. (above) A study by Dorothea Lange of migrants who had headed west from the dustbowl of Oklahoma and were photographed camping by the roadside at Blythe, California, in August 1936.

Photographs such as these seemed to indict an apparently failed system. By the late 1930s a dreadful plague of unemployment had settled on most of the industrialised world. Tens of millions of people became jobless and many families were made homeless, affecting their ability to feed themselves adequately, which led to increased illness and disease. It took a world war to bring relief.

The importance of education... (top) A debate on democracy at Cheadle High School, 13 November 1939. (above) A Nazi lesson in strategy – the importance of Danzig to Germany, September 1938. (right) A study in British class distinction – two Eton schoolboys are appraised by three young Cockneys outside Lord's, June 1937.

The unemployed... (clockwise, from the top) A member of the National Unemployed Workers'
Movement is removed from his protest at Stepney Employment Exchange, 11 January 1939.
A mean street, c.1935. Men seeking work, 21 January 1939.

The wheels of industry. (clockwise, from above) In Cardiff putting the finishing touches to baskets for South African oil cake, 16 May 1938. Repairing station clocks for the Great Western Railway, Reading, 1934. Mr Burns shapes a boater for a Harrow School pupil, 18 February 1930 – the original was designed by his grandmother. Burring and sanding dartboards, 2 December 1937.

(top) Hikers in the Lake District meet a shepherd and his dog, 1935. (above) Hi-tech camping, 1930 – the couple have the latest portable gramophone. (opposite) Unexpected thrills on the rollercoaster at Southend Fair, 8 October 1938.

(above) Young members of the Locomotive Sports Club parade through Red Square in star formation, c.1937. (right) German gymnasts in good (and New) order at the Berlin Olympics, August 1936.

The Berlin Olympic Games drew record crowds and receipts. Although the event witnessed sixteen new world records, it will always be remembered for two men and their performances. One was an athlete, African-American Jesse Owens who won four gold medals. The other was a politician, Führer Adolf Hitler whose racism meant he refused to recognise Owens' achievements and left the stadium early to avoid having to meet him.

The Spanish Civil War. (top) Captured Republicans on the Samosierra Front, November 1936. (above) Republican snipers, *c.*1936. (opposite) Refugees arrive in Valencia, *c.*1937.

(above) The devastating fire at the Crystal Palace, 1 December 1936. (right) The *Hindenburg* disaster, Lakehurst, New Jersey, 6 May 1937.

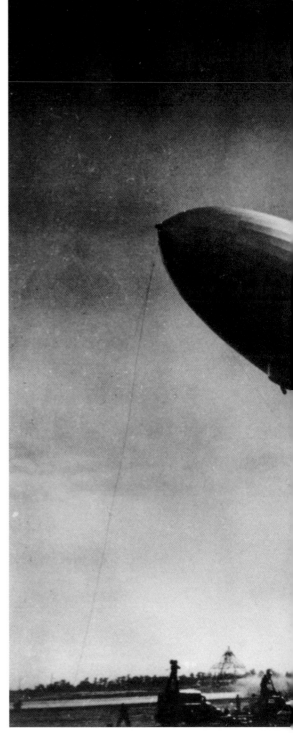

The end for the graceful, passenger-carrying airships came in New Jersey at the Naval Air Station, Lakehurst, just after 7.20pm. As the Hindenburg *dropped her mooring lines, there was a flash and an explosion as hundreds of thousands of cubic feet of hydrogen caught fire. Within minutes the ship was a molten tangle of twisted aluminium. Thirty-three people died: amazingly, more than sixty survived.*

In the second week of the war, the Duke and Duchess of Windsor pay a hurried visit from France to Sussex, 13 September 1939.

King Edward VIII abdicated the British throne because he chose to love a twice-divorced American commoner rather than fulfil his duty to the nation. The matter was in fact a little more complicated. Churchill tried to raise a King's Party to save him, but The Times *and the Archbishop of Canterbury were determined that he should go. In the end, only Hitler really wished to see Edward restored.*

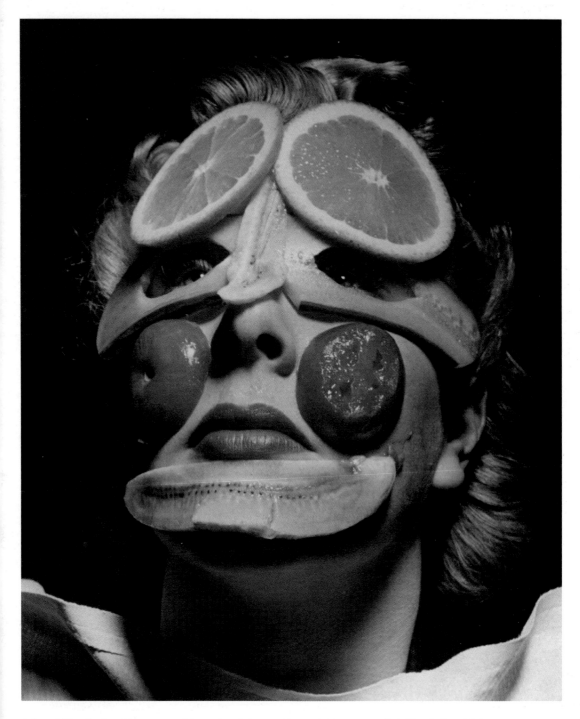

(above) The fruits of beauty... skin moisturising in March 1939. (opposite) The fruits of labour...
A bed-maker at the University of Cambridge enjoys a tea break, 3 June 1939.

Gods and goddesses of the silver screen... (top) James Stewart (left) and Henry Fonda at Slapsy Maxie's Café, c.1938. (above) Sasha's 1935 portrait of Vivien Leigh, who was already a star on the stage, but not yet on screen.

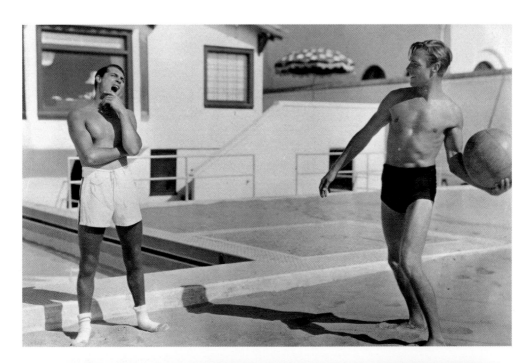

(top) Debonair Cary Grant and Randolph Scott (with the ball) by the poolside of their Santa Monica seafront home, *c*.1935. (above) A publicity still released by MGM for *Gone With The Wind*, which starred Clark Gable, seen here reading the novel, in the lead role, *c*.1939.

Reaching for culture. (top) Hitler and Goebbels at the Day of Art Exhibition, Munich, 11 July 1938. (above) Hanging Max Beckmann's *Temptation* at New Burlington Galleries, 4 July 1938. (opposite) Jacob Epstein and *Genesis*, 1931.

(above) A tragic moment in the life of Czechoslovakia. German troops receive the Nazi salute as they enter Prague, October 1938. (opposite, top) Neville Chamberlain declares 'it is peace in our time', Heston Aerodrome, September 1938. (opposite, bottom) The axis of evil: the Führer and the Duce meet in Florence, May 1938.

The Munich Crisis was the final fruitless act in the process of appeasement towards Hitler's territorial ravages. The British Prime Minister flew to Munich for talks with Hitler, Mussolini, and Daladier of France on the future of the Sudetenland area of Czechoslovakia. Britain and France capitulated. After hours of talks Hitler had his way. Chamberlain flew back to London where he was greeted as a hero. One year later, the Nazis invaded Poland, and Europe went to war.

(previous page) A Fleet Air Arm 'scramble'. (above) The morning after a terrifying night... Balham High Street, London, 17 October 1940. (opposite) Londoners shelter from the nightly bombing at Piccadilly Circus underground, 1940.

During the London Blitz, the Luftwaffe dropped 100 tons of high-explosive bombs every night from 7 September to 2 November 1940. Three years later, the RAF were dropping 1,600 tons a night on Germany's cities.

Despite the destruction, it's business as usual. (above) Early morning deliveries on 9 October 1940 and early morning collections on 11 September 1940. (opposite) Never mind the mess: the bride steps out on 5 November 1940.

Means of defence. (clockwise, from the top) An air-raid shelter for one, Marlborough House, London. A gas-masked policeman in Gloucester, March 1941. Mine games on the east coast of England, February 1940.

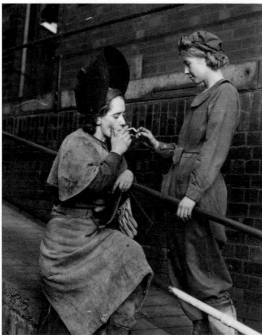

Safety first. (clockwise, from the top) Under the mistletoe, 1940s' style. A mother holds a gas mask designed for babies. War meant new roles for women – two take a break at the steel mill, November 1942.

(above) The Warsaw ghetto after the uprising
of 1943. (right) The Nazi Youth Group in Berlin,
c.1940. (opposite) Children in an indoor bomb
shelter, Wembley, North London, 1941.

*People left home in wartime for a variety
of reasons. Both men and women were con-
scripted for national service in the forces,
in the mines and in the factories. In Nazi
Germany youths went to camps, where they
were prepared for tougher duties to come.
Those deemed to be enemies of the Nazi
state – Jews and Slavs, gypsies and
Communists – were deported into ghettos
and concentration camps. In the United
Kingdom thousands of families spent their
nights in shelters as the bombs rained down.*

(previous page) Roosevelt's 'day of infamy'... The USS *Shaw* explodes during the Imperial Japanese Air Force's raid on the Naval Air Station at Pearl Harbor, 7 December 1941.(above) A coral reef at Okinawa is destroyed to provide a landing place for US supply ships, 1945. (opposite) A wounded Soviet officer issues orders on the Eastern Front during the Great Patriotic War, *c.*1941.

(above) The latest of the Mohicans – an *al fresco* barber shop for American paratroopers, Arras, 23 March 1945. (opposite) *'Blister-krieg'* – a foot inspection for British troops in the North African desert, *c*.1943.

A time out of war... Somewhere in the south of England, American GIs await the big order for the invasion of France, June 1944.

It was one of the best-kept secrets of the war. Everyone speculated, but only a handful knew where the invasion of Nazi-occupied Europe was going to take place. It could have been southern France, on the Mediterranean or Atlantic coasts; and it could have been on the Channel coast east of the River Seine. The build-up was colossal: 1,200 fighting ships, 4,000 assault craft, 1,600 merchant vessels, 13,000 aircraft and more than three million men.

Invasion. (top) American soldiers in the Pacific, 1942. (above) Sicily, July 1943. (right) Carentan, Normandy, 11 July 1944.

'Next to a battle lost...' (above) Soviet infantrymen at the epic Battle of Stalingrad in 1943. (opposite) In July 1943 a German soldier holds his head in despair at the Battle of Kursk, while a dead comrade lies nearby.

The stars go to war. (opposite) Captain Clark Gable trains bomber crews in Britain, July 1943. (top) Marlene Dietrich returns to New York after a 500-show tour for US troops, August 1945. (above) Dancer Josephine Baker at a VE Party, 2 June 1945.

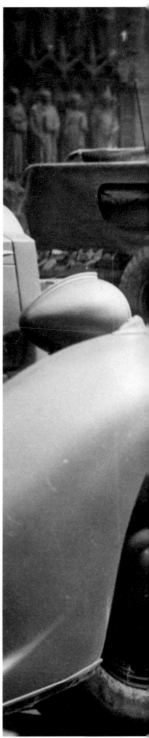

The liberation of Paris, August 1944. (top) Parisians cheer French and
American troops. (above) A French soldier guards German POWs. (right)
Sheltering as hidden sniper fire breaks out.

*For two weeks Paris had been restless. Collaborators were rounded
up, and some were shot. Railwaymen and policemen went on
strike. Then, on 25 August, General Leclerc and a French armoured
division entered the city, and four years of occupation were over.*

Settling scores. (above) The public humiliation of Frenchwomen accused of 'collaborating' with German troops, 1945. (opposite) A German POW runs a gauntlet of hatred at the hands of an angry mob in Toulon, *c.*1945.

France was not in a forgiving mood in the wake of the Nazi defeats in the summer of 1944. Those who had aided, entertained or too eagerly done business with the occupying Germans received short shrift, with women the particular targets of a vindictive public. Pétain, head of the government of Vichy France, was executed. Many French collaborators were murdered and pictures such as these shocked the world. Soon, wiser counsels began to prevail.

The essence of inhumanity. (above) A liberated Russian slave labourer denounces his Nazi guard, 14 April 1945. (right) Belsen, April 1945.

Whether it is remembered as the Holocaust or the Final Solution, no words can adequately convey the full horror of what was carried out in Nazi factories of extermination set up in occupied Europe. A dark, destructive evil entered the soul of guards, commandants, doctors and scientists alike, which resulted in millions of human beings being sent to unspeakable deaths.

Victory in Europe. (clockwise, from the top) US paratroopers pose with a Nazi trophy in Normandy, June 1944. The flag of the USSR is run up over the Reichstag, 30 April 1945. American and Soviet soldiers join hands across the River Elbe, 27 April 1945.

While troops from the various Allied armies celebrated victory, their political leaders were already squabbling over the spoils of war. Soviet troops had won the race for Berlin, and by so doing the USSR obtained control over much of eastern Europe for the next 45 years.

(clockwise, from top left) Rebuilding Dresden, 1946. Refugees in Berlin, 1945. Hard 'bargaining', 1945. Fraternisation, July 1945. (opposite) An orphan tries to buy cigarettes with his late father's Iron Cross.

The end of the war was a time of desperate need in war-damaged Europe. People offered valuable personal possessions – and even their bodies – in exchange for food, clothes or cigarettes. Most occupying troops behaved well, though there were misunderstandings – and with an absence of local young men, the tender shoots of relationships sprouted out of soldier-civilian fraternisation.

(opposite) Colonel Paul Tibbets, Junior, prepares to take-off in his B-29 bomber – it was 6 August 1945 and his destination was Hiroshima. (above) Mamoru Shigemitsu, Japan's Foreign Minister, and General Richard Sutherland sign the surrender document, 2 September 1945.

Home are the heroes... (above) Gunner Hector Murdoch is greeted by his family
outside their new 'prefab' in Tulse Hill, South London, 15 October 1945.
(opposite) A mother greets her demobbed WAAF daughter, 10 September 1945.

*It was the moment that men, women and children had longed for
during their struggles and suffering: a time of family reunion,
when fathers could meet children they might never have seen
before. For many it was the most important event of the war, but
for a few it was an anti-climax and a prelude to disenchantment.*

The birth of Israel. (clockwise, from opposite) Jewish refugees arrive in Cyprus on their way to Palestine, 1947. A young Jewish woman arrives in Haifa, c.1947. Refugees wade ashore at Nahariya after evading the British blockade, 2 February 1948.

The Jitterbug. (above, left) Cutting a rug at a *palais de danse*, November 1949. (above, right) Parisian students hit the timbers in their sneakers, March 1949. (opposite) Bopping at Club Eleven, 1949.

Along with chewing gum, Lucky Strikes, nylons and their libido, the American GIs brought the art of jiving to the dance floors of Europe. Local youth seized on its snaky athleticism with uncon- fined enthusiasm. In its various forms jive became the dance craze of the 1940s, condemned only by those too old to try it.

(above) This Bill Brandt fashion shot in July 1948 contains all the ingredients for a happy holiday: sunshine, swimwear, wine, camera and parasol. (opposite) The shocking new bikini modelled at the Molitor Pool, Paris, July 1946.

The war had ended and holidays were possible again. For most people these were simple affairs – day trips to the coast or the countryside, or at best a weekend in a seaside resort. Beaches were laboriously cleared of mines and rusting barbed-wire was dragged from the dunes. Piers were rebuilt. Ice creams reappeared. And the blue skies were at last clear of enemy aircraft and rockets.

Artists and craftsmen... (above) The British sculptor Henry Moore at work on a female figure, *c*.1948. (opposite) Pablo Picasso makes a delivery of pottery to a Paris exhibition, *c*.1948.

Creator and creations. (opposite) Christian Dior, inventor of the elegant 'New Look', with two of his models, 1949. (above) The 'New Look' reaches London, marking an end to wartime austerity and a return to fashion luxury.

(previous page) Light fades as US Marines struggle ashore during the assault on Inchon, a key stage of the Korean War, 14 September 1950. 7 October 1950. (opposite) Korean civilians with a casualty search for a US medical officer to provide some treatment. (above) South Korean prisoners, suspected of North Korean sympathies, await interrogation.

'Why the North Koreans did not resist more forcefully, I do not know... They lost their beachhead, they lost their lives, and with them the lives of many simple people who had the ill-luck to live in places which people in war rooms decided to smash...' – journalist James Cameron.

THE TORY TEAM

CHURCHILL

Cut out Government waste
VOTE CONSERVATIVE

Turn hopes into Homes
VOTE CONSERVATIVE

CHURCH
COMMI
ROOM

WINSTON
HURCHILL
...er of the Conservative and Unionist Party

Old campaigner, new campaigner. (opposite) Winston Churchill gives the 'Victory' sign from his election HQ at South Woodford, 6 October 1951. He won. (above) Young pretender Margaret Roberts (later better known as Prime Minister Thatcher) canvasses in Dartford. She lost.

A nation mourns... (above) Crowds gather outside Buckingham Palace, 6 February 1952. (right) Daughter, mother and widow attend the funeral of King George VI, 15 February 1952.

He was the king who had ascended reluctantly to the throne vacated by his brother, Edward, who had abdicated in 1936. George led his people through the war and had loved his family openly. His death was mourned across the realm.

(opposite) The crowning moment at the coronation of Queen Elizabeth II, Westminster Abbey, 2 June 1953.
(above) August 1952 – children in Stepney, East London, learn of a party to be held in ten months' time.

The BOAC de Haviland Comet prepares for its inaugural flight to Johannesburg from London's Heathrow Airport, 2 May 1952.

The Comet was the world's first jet airliner. It was sleek and exceptionally fast, but a series of crashes led to its withdrawal from service later in the 1950s. Nevertheless it sparked a revolution in air travel: flights became cheaper, more frequent, and more comfortable. Passenger numbers increased at a supersonic pace.

Still the fashion capital of the world... (above) An ensemble by **Fath**, based on Dior's A-line design, 25 April 1955. (opposite) An evening gown by **Balenciaga**, 23 April 1955.

Makers of the Cuban Revolution. (above) Fidel Castro at a sugar plantation near Havana, shortly after his release from jail, 1955. (opposite) Ernesto Che Guevara at the Battle of Santa Clara, 1958.

In March 1952 Fulgencio Batista staged a military coup in Cuba. Over the next seven years resistance to his corrupt and murderous regime grew, until on 1 January 1959 Batista fled, with US$40 million of government funds. Fidel Castro's army of revolutionaries entered Santiago de Cuba, while Guevara's force entered Havana.

The Hungarian Rising of October and November 1956. (clockwise, from the top) Bodies of secret policemen in the street. A 15-year-old freedom fighter. Patriots burn Stalin's portrait. Soviet T-55 tanks in Budapest.

The Suez Crisis. (clockwise, from above) Egyptian children train to defend their country, September 1956. Distress on the streets of Port Said, 8 November 1956. A sentry at the British headquarters at Ishmailiya; an Egyptian looks on.

In 1956 Britain and the United States withdrew funds for the building of the Aswan Dam in Egypt. President Nasser then took control of the Suez Canal. Against the advice of the United States and the United Nations, France, Britain and Israel responded by invading Egypt. Militarily, the action was a success, but politically it was a disaster. In the face of worldwide condemnation, the invaders were forced to withdraw.

Demonstrating, exploding, exploiting…
(above) Marchers from the Campaign for Nuclear
Disarmament en route from Aldermaston to
London, 6 April 1958. (opposite) Testing the atom
bomb on the Yucca Flats, Nevada, 8 May 1945.
(right) Studying the possible applications of nuclear
power at the University of Michigan, c.1955.

*There were those who believed in the
nuclear deterrent, and those who cam-
paigned vigorously to 'Ban the Bomb'. Not
since the Depression of the 1930s had so
many people been on a march. It was a
clash of ideas and ideals. Caught in the
middle was the silent majority.*

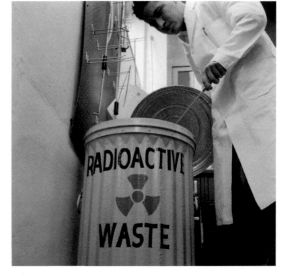

(above) Pyrogen tests in a chemical research centre, *c.*1956. (right) Giant dentures used to demonstrate brushing techniques, *c.*1950.

It was the last unchallenged age of experimental science. God had given man – and most scientists were men in the 1950s – dominion over animals, and if that led to suffering on their part so that people could gain relief, so be it. A later age was to have more difficulty swallowing this philosophy than the drugs that resulted from it.

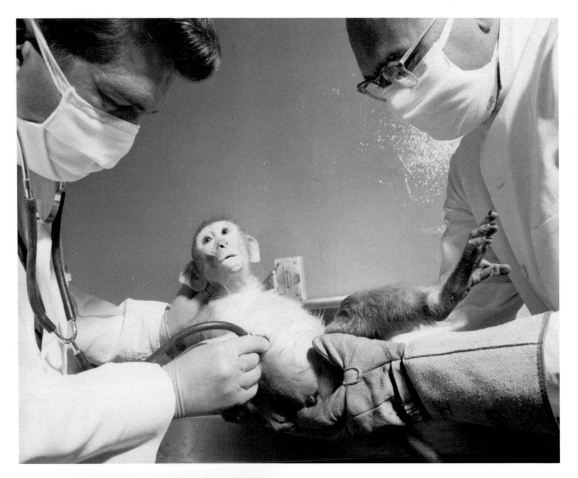

(above) A monkey's heartbeat is checked before a drug test, c.1956. (left) Eye tests with a metronoscope, New York, c.1955.

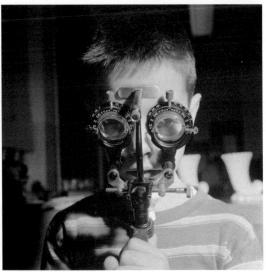

Young Japanese men celebrate the festival of *hadaka matsuri* in the Saidaiji Temple, Okayama, c.1946.

Hadaka matsuri *marks the lunar New Year and takes place in complete darkness (the photograph was taken by flashlight). Naked men leap into a pulsating crowd of other naked men, and the search begins to find two camphor-scented batons thrown into this pit of seething humanity.*

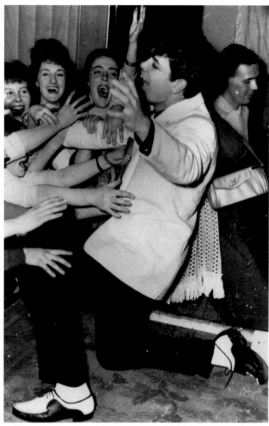

Rock idols. (above, left) Tommy Steele – aka Hicks – in his Steelmen days,
February 1957. (above, right) Nineteen-year-old Cliff Richard and fans,
10 February 1959. (opposite) Bill Haley and his Comets at the Dominion
Theatre, Tottenham Court Road, London, 7 February 1957.

*Bill Haley was a hillbilly singer from Chester, Pennsylvania. When
he made his first record,* Rock the Joint, *in 1952, the world wasn't
quite ready for rock 'n' roll. Three years later, it was. Bill Haley
and his Comets exploded onto the music scene with* Rock Around
the Clock. *Fans went wild. Audiences erupted. Teenagers screamed.
Clerics condemned. But the beat went on... and on... and on...*

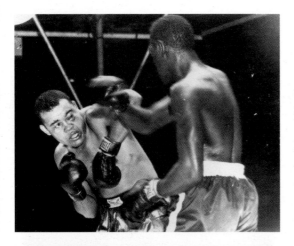

(clockwise, from opposite) Apprentices spar at the British Railways depot, Kentish Town, London, January 1950. Joe Louis (left) and Ezzard Charles, September 1950. Sugar Ray Robinson (right) and Randolph Turpin, September 1951. The young Kray twins, 26 February 1952. Jim (left) and Henry Cooper, 17 November 1954.

Boxing 'packed a punch' at the ticket office in the 1950s. Crowds flocked to see Louis fail to win back the World Heavyweight title from Charles at the Yankee Stadium in New York, and to see Robinson regain his title from Turpin at the Polo Ground. Most people tended to avoid the Kray twins and their less than noble art in London's East End. Henry Cooper's bout of glory was yet to come.

(top) Enesco – the Romanian violinist and compos-
er teaches at Bryanston, 1953. (above) Maestro –
Stravinsky conducts, 1959. (opposite) Satchmo –
Louis Armstrong, 1956.

(clockwise, from opposite) An assistant bites a loose thread from Joan Crawford's dress, July 1956. Arthur Miller and Marilyn Monroe on honeymoon, 17 July 1956. Vivien Leigh and Laurence Olivier arrive unostentatiously at Rome Airport, February 1953.

(above) Sizing up the opposition… Sun-burnt holiday-makers at a bar on Corfu,
30 October 1954. (opposite) Sheltering from the wind by the Wannsee Lake, Berlin,
24 May 1958.

On the street... (opposite) Police search a black Londoner in Talbot Road during the Notting Hill race riots, September 1958. (above) On the buses... A London bus conductor of the 1950s.

During the war the call had gone out for black citizens of the Commonwealth to fight for the Mother Country. After the war, the same subjects were invited to Britain to ease the labour shortage. Of those who responded, many had left friends and families to come and live and work in an often cold, grey and unwelcoming land filled with strangers, where employers wanted them but some landlords and landladies made it clear that they didn't.

(previous page) The Thin Blue Line bulges but doesn't break as Beatles fans wait for their beloved idols to collect MBEs at Buckingham Palace, 26 October 1965. (right) Bodies litter the streets of Sharpeville after the South African township massacre of 21 March 1960. Most have been shot in the back.

The Pan-Africanist Congress in South Africa had organised a day of peaceful protest against the hated Pass Laws. Five thousand residents of Sharpeville marched to the local police headquarters to give themselves up voluntarily. Without warning, police opened fire. Sixty-seven protesters were killed and 186 were wounded. It was a watershed event in South African affairs and drew the world's attention to the brutality of apartheid.

(opposite) Dr Hendrik Verwoerd, Prime Minister of South Africa, and his wife leave Cape Town for London, 27 February 1961 – five years later he was assassinated. (right) Nelson and Winnie Mandela, c.1962 – two years later he was sentenced to life imprisonment.

Twist and shout... (above) A couple 'doing the Twist', 1961. (opposite) An Australian Mod in a classic parka stomps the night away with his girlfriend in a Sydney club, 11 September 1963.

Spot the real masks... (opposite) US President John F. Kennedy and Soviet Premier Nikita Khrushchev meet for talks in Vienna, 3 June 1961. (above) Anti-nuclear protesters in New York, 3 November 1961.

After the failure of an earlier Paris summit, negotiations between the USA and the USSR in Vienna were relatively fruitful. There was a 'frank' exchange on the subjects of Berlin and Laos, and the world breathed a sigh of relief that the two superpowers were once again on speaking terms.

A strange tourist hotspot in Germany in the 1960s... Sightseers stop off during a city tour to inspect the Berlin Wall, 19 February 1964.

The Berlin Wall first appeared in August 1961. At first it was a shoddy obstacle of cement blocks and barbed wire, hastily erected to prevent Berliners from the Eastern Sector migrating to the Western Sector. It quickly became a focal point in the Cold War – a powerful symbol of the contest between capitalism and communism, and a poignant place of death and despair.

Protest and arrest. (above) Supporters of CND (the Campaign for Nuclear Disarmament) marching from Aldermaston, Easter (March) 1963. (opposite) Police remove sit-down protesters from Parliament Square, 24 March 1962.

In 1949, the British Army Journal *advised that 'the best defence against the atom bomb is not to be there when it goes off'. To millions of men and women in CND, it made more sense simply to Ban the Bomb – and so they marched each year, in the hope that the world would come to its senses.*

(above) The presidential motorcade heads towards the book depository and the grassy knoll, Dallas, 22 November 1963. (right) John F. Kennedy's brothers, his widow, daughter and son at his funeral, Washington, DC, 25 November 1963.

Very few people know why the assassination happened, and perhaps even who really did it, but most of the world has seen the grainy images of President Kennedy rocking forward and back, his wife frantically trying to nurse him and then the limousine accelerating through downtown Dallas on a hopeless mission to Parkland Memorial Hospital...

(top and above) Five personalities of the year – Prime Minister Harold Wilson and The Beatles, 19 March 1964. (right) Nothing left to imagine – John Lennon and Yoko Ono, c.1968.

(clockwise, from top left) Catherine Deneuve and
David Bailey; Roman Polanski and Sharon Tate;
Jane Fonda and Alain Delon; Federico Fellini;
Luchino Visconti; Ursula Andress and Woody Allen.

*Despite the presence of considerable cine-
matic talent in the 1960s, the film industry
suffered. Hollywood chose to throw money
at the problem and financed a series of
blockbusting epics –* Ben Hur, El Cid *and*
Cleopatra. *And then, just like the US
Cavalry in the films of old, James Bond
arrived in the nick of time...*

(clockwise, from top left) A Paco Rabanne leather coat, 1967. Mary Quant, November 1966. Jean Shrimpton, her hair styled by Carita, in October 1965. Twiggy, May 1966. Simply gorgeous, March 1966.

(previous page) The Rolling Stones at full blast before an audience of 150,000 at the Knebworth Festival, Hertfordshire, 1967. (above) 'Stone style' – a dressed-for-the-dock Brian Jones outside West London Magistrates Court, June 1967. (opposite) Beatle boutique – smartly besuited Paul McCartney and John Lennon (left) arrive at Heathrow Airport, May 1968.

(above) The great victory... Bobby Moore holds aloft the Jules Rimet trophy at Wembley Stadium, 30 July 1966. (opposite) The Greatest... Cassius Clay (later better known as Muhammad Ali) after defeating Sonny Liston, 25 March 1964.

Experienced sports writers had written off Clay's chances of winning the title, and this had riled the 22-year-old challenger. When Liston decided to quit after six rounds, Clay floated across the ring, yelling to them: 'eat your words.' But only three of the 46 who had predicted Clay's defeat were present at ringside.

(above) Mao Zedong reads his own published thoughts in a Chinese newspaper, 1963. (opposite) Demonstrators outside the Chinese Embassy in London, 1967.

The Little Red Book *and the* Thoughts of Chairman Mao *were that rare phenomenon – a political best-seller. Inside China, the books were compulsory reading, but even in the world outside the texts were bought in large quantities.*

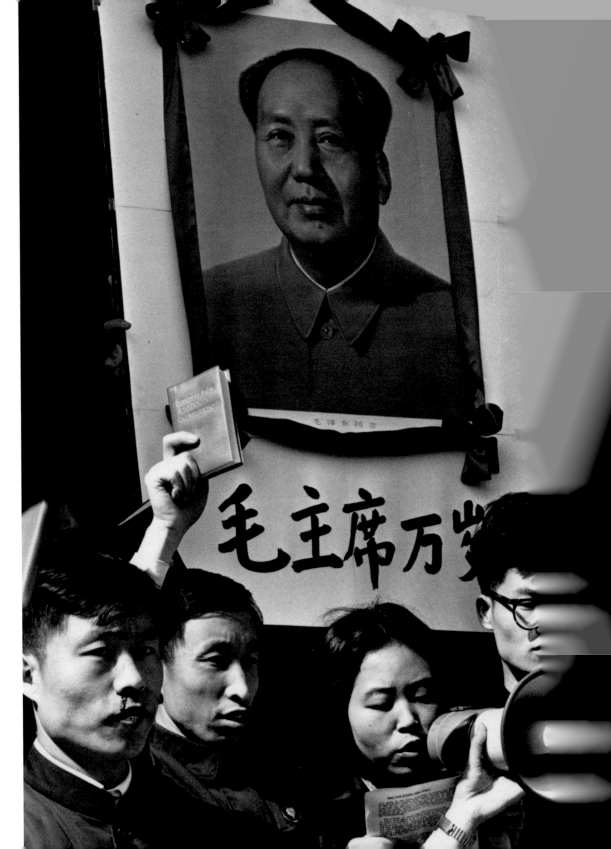

Israel Defence Force mechanised infantry units passing Egyptian POWs as they move up to the Suez front during the Six-Day War, 9 June 1967.

Another French Revolution. (clockwise, from the top) Student leader Daniel Cohn-Bendit at the Gare de l'Est, Paris, 14 May 1968. A lone policeman puts his faith in tear gas. The Tricolor is waved from the Arc de Triomphe.

Searing soul... (above) Marsha Hunt at full throttle, September 1969. (opposite) Joe Cocker rasps it out to the Isle of Wight, 11 September 1969.

No decade, save perhaps the 1930s, can match the 1960s for the
quality and breadth of its musical output – Elvis, The Beatles, The
Rolling Stones, the Everlys, The Beach Boys, The Doors, Sonny and
Cher, Marvin Gaye and the Tamla Motown sound, The Crystals,
The Supremes, The Animals, The Bee Gees, Buddy Holly, Jimi
Hendrix, Bob Dylan, Jerry Lee... and dozens more. Music revivals
may come and go, but the sounds of the 1960s live for ever.

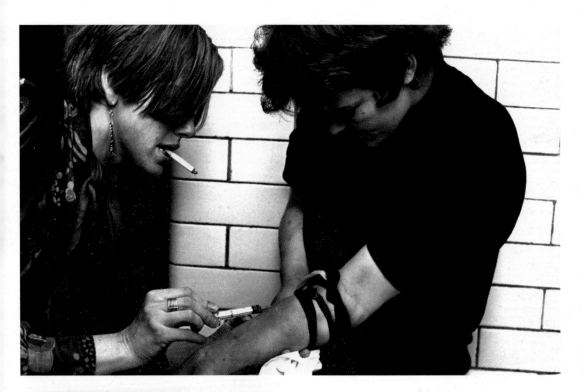

Class of '69. (clockwise, from opposite) A Rolling Stones fan in Hyde Park, London, 5 July. 'Jacking up' in Piccadilly Circus, 6 October. The early days of Flower Power, 20 September.

For the young and unattached the so-called Swinging Sixties was a time of free love, cheap dope and pricey clothes. There was music everywhere: on pirate radio stations, at concerts in the park, on LPs and singles. And there was a growing market in the ugly underworld of hard drugs.

(below) Apollo 11 blasts off from Pad 39A at the Kennedy Space Center, 16 July 1969. (opposite) Four days later and 'the Eagle has landed', with the first human footprint being made on the moon, accompanied by the immortal words – '... one small step for man, one giant leap for mankind...'

(previous page) Toasting the talks. Soviet Premier Leonid Brezhnev (second from left) and US President Gerald Ford raise their glasses at the dinner that concluded the Strategic Arms Limitation Treaty (SALT) talks, Vladivostok, 24 November 1974. (clockwise, from the top) A world at war: The Yom Kippur War, October 1973. A South Vietnamese soldier, January 1973. Indian Mukti guerrillas execute Bengalis accused of collaboration with Pakistan, 1971.

Some wars were revivals – Yom Kippur was a rerun of Israel-Arab conflicts of previous decades; others were hangovers – the Vietnam War had burnt its way through the 1950s, 1960s and into the 1970s; and a few were newcomers – among them the struggle for Bangladeshi independence.

Bodyguards maintain a protective lookout for President Salvador Allende of Chile, 11 September 1973. Ten days later, Allende was dead and General Augusto Pinochet Ugarte had taken control.

The coup in September 1973 was not the first attempt in the recent history of Chile to drive the elected president from office. In 1972 US business interests had backed a 'bosses' strike, which was defeated when the workers took control of the factories. In June 1973 a split in the armed forces delayed a military coup, but three months later Pinochet and the CIA had their way.

War games. (clockwise, from the top) Soldiers from a Scottish regiment and Belfast locals, 20 April 1971. A doughty Ulster warrior, *c.*1970. A burnt-out playground, Belfast, *c.*1975.

Fake weapons, real wounds. (opposite, top) Chinese schoolchildren practising military-style exercises with wooden rifles, Hanking, April 1974. (opposite, bottom) Le Luy (right), 10 years old, and Cu Van Anh, just six years old, both victims of the Vietnam War, February 1973. (right) A child soldier of the Marxist MPLA (Movimento Popular de Libertação de Angola), Angola, February 1976.

The hand of dedication... Watched by his wife Betty, Chief Justice Warren Berger (left) administers the presidential oath to Gerald Ford on 13 August 1974 in the wake of the resignation of Richard Nixon.

Richard Nixon was the first US President to resign. Congress withdrew support for him after he admitted withholding information and making misleading statements in the wake of the Watergate blunder. His own glib (and forked) tongue had helped to bring him down, but it was perhaps his untrustworthy body language that most betrayed him.

The thumb of resignation... Richard Nixon quits the White House as his son-in-law, David Eisenhower, looks on, 9 August 1974.

(left) Jacques Chirac, later to become president of France, addresses the assembly of the UDR party, c.1975 – in the shadow of General de Gaulle.

(right) Helmut Kohl, later to become chancellor of a reunified Germany, basks in the reflected glory of Konrad Adenauer after being re-elected to the national Chair of the CDU party, 17 July 1975.

Svelte '70s. (clockwise, from opposite) Christian Dior furs, 1976; John Bates knitwear, *c.*1974; Mary Quant lollipop, 1971; St Tropez chic, 1972; and Gingham platforms, 1972.

Flares and flauntings. (clockwise, from above)
An American hippy in London, *c*.1972; Kansai
Yamamoto's woollen jumpsuit, 1971; Susan Shaw
in an eye-catching mini skirt, 1975; an enticing
T-shirt offer, 1975.

Designer terrorists. (above) Palestinian hijacker Leila Khaled in a refugee camp, Beirut, 1975.
(opposite) Heiress Patty Hearst is caught on surveillance camera working for her former kidnap-
pers in the Symbionese Liberation Army, 19 September 1975.

The Baader-Meinhof
gang. (left) Ulrike
Meinhof, joint head of
West Germany's Red
Army Faction, is arrest-
ed, 19 June 1972.
(above) Hans-Martin
Schleyer, president of
the German Employers'
Association in RAF
hands, 6 September
1977 – he was later
killed. (opposite)
Andreas Baader, the
other half of the lead-
ership,
31 January 1972.

(opposite) A Dutch hostage held prisoner by Moluccan separatist terrorists in the Indonesian Consulate, Amsterdam, 1975. (above) A masked killer from the Black September gang that attacked the Munich Olympic Village during the games held in the city, 7 September 1972.

A hippie wedding at the Watchfield Pop Festival, Oxfordshire, August 1975. Naked guests enjoy the bizarre ceremony, while bride and groom – daubed with tiger balm – hide behind a tambourine. They had known each other for 48 hours.

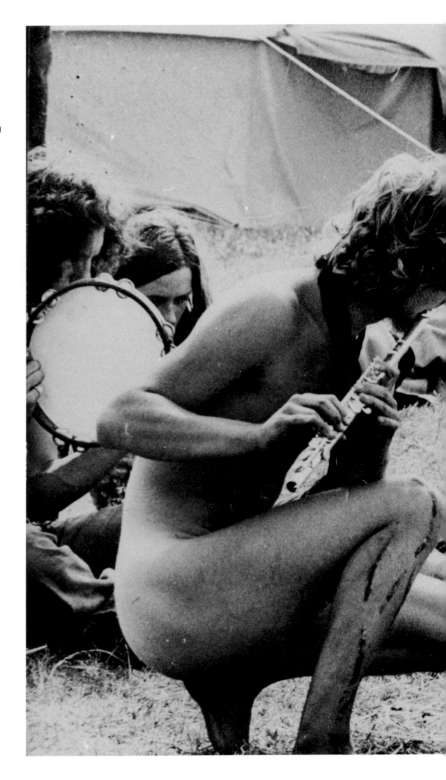

Top talent. (above) Mick Jagger, 1976. (left) David Bowie's last appearance as Ziggy Stardust, 1973. (opposite) Tina Turner's first solo concert, 1978.

It was a multi-faceted musical age: one of the supergroup (The Who, Cream, ELP); punk (Blondie, The Ramones, The Sex Pistols); Abba; 'glam-rock' (David Bowie and Marc Bolan); family entertainment (The Jackson Five, The Osmonds); the incredibly high-pitched disco sound of The Bee Gees; and of Elvis's retirement. All of it was wonderful.

(top) Crazy horses... The Osmonds sock it to their Swedish fans in Stockholm, July 1975.
(above) ABC... The Jackson Five, plus Randy (third from the left) makes six, October 1972.

(top) Five years on from Waterloo... Abba, live in concert, 20 February 1979.
(above) 'We don't make music, we make chaos...' The Sex Pistols, 3 December 1976.

Admiration and hatred. (above) A pierced punk fan at a concer t by The Clash in Stockholm, 17 June 1977. (opposite) A member of the neo-fascist British Movement is arrested, c.1975.

Punks and Skins. (above) A fan bearing the slogan 'No Future' on her forehead – possibly a touch of self-deprecating humour, but then again perhaps not – attends a London gig featuring The Jam and The Clash, May 1977. (right) A punk's bum-flap sends a typically nihilistic message to mainstream society, the Roxy nightclub, London, March 1978. (opposite) One of the angry young men who made up the Skinhead movement of the 1970s, photographed in 1978.

Hamming it up... (above) Debbie Harry of Blondie, November 1977. (right) Pop star Elton John leads out the Watford footballing hopefuls, April 1974. (opposite) Elvis Costello and his Fender guitar, 1977.

(above) Obstructing the members' view... Greg Chappel puts bat to balls during the World Cricket Series in Brisbane, December 1979. (opposite) Just missing the stump... Lord's, London, September 1977.

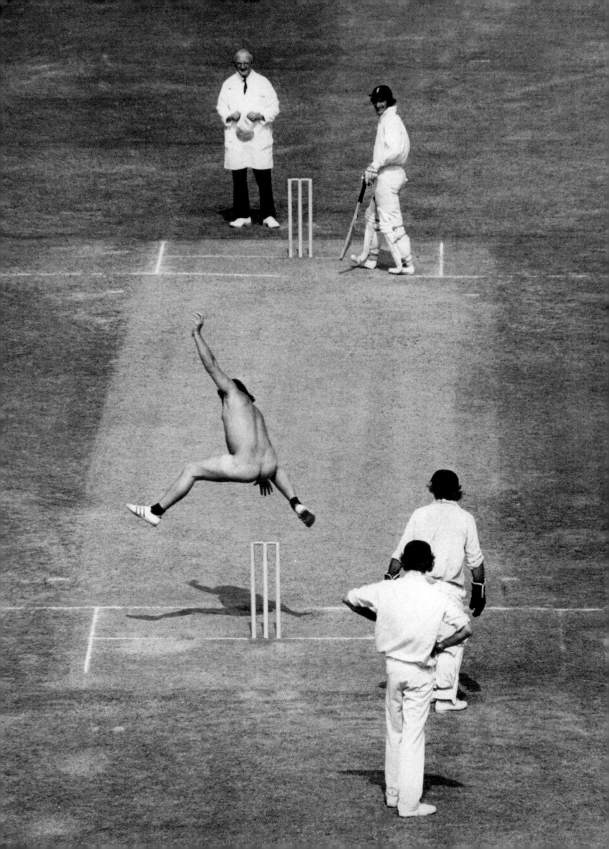

Court favourites... (clockwise, from the top) Chris Evert, 1973; Tracy Austin, 1979; Ilie Nastase, 1978; Martina Navratilova on her way to winning the Wimbledon Singles Championship, 1979.

(clockwise, from the top) Andy Warhol and his *Princess of Iran*, 1977; Bridget Riley and *oeuvre*, 1979; Allen Jones and the human coffee table, 1972; a worse-for-wear Francis Bacon receives upright support from scaffolding, 1970.

Men behind the camera... (clockwise, from above) Clint
Eastwood on location for *Breezy*; Stanley Kubrick on set,
1971; Sylvester Stallone making *Paradise Alley*; Sergio
Leone, of Spaghetti Western fame, sports toy guns at
table, 1973.

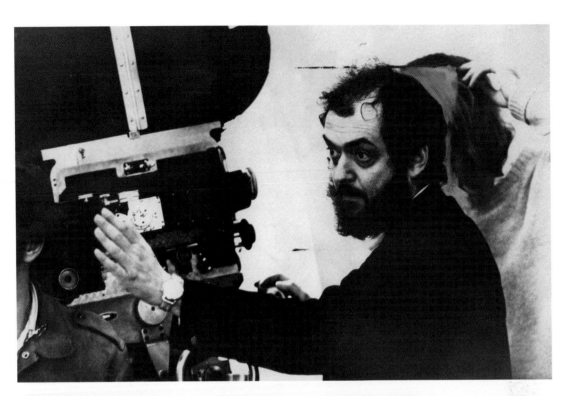

(opposite) Nobel Prize-winner Alexander Solzhenitsyn admires the coastline of Norway in 1974 – the year he was deported from the USSR. (above) Dancer Mikhail Baryshnikov in 1975 – the year after his defection from the USSR.

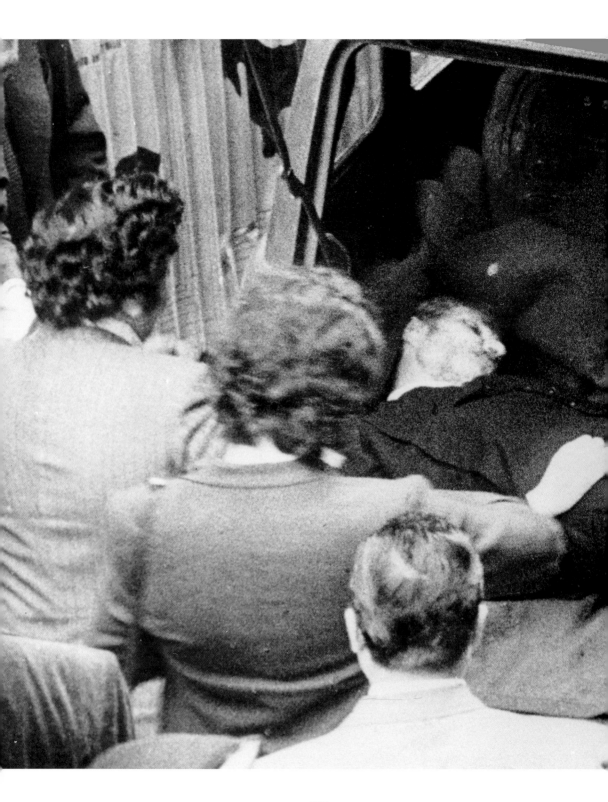

The body of Italy's former premier Aldo Moro, found in the boot of a car in the Via Caetani, Rome, 16 March 1978. He had been kidnapped and executed by the Red Brigade.

Defenders of the faiths. (above) Pope John Paul II arrives in Madrid – he was the first non-Italian pope elected for 450 years. (opposite) Ayatollah Ruhollah Khomeini in December 1978 – two months before his triumphant return to Iran after having been in exile.

Women members of the Iranian militia take part in the siege of the US Embassy in Tehran, two weeks after Ayatollah Khomeini's return.

In January 1979 the Shah of Iran fled after 37 years as the country's ruler. A few days later Prime Minister Shahpur Bakhtiar gave permission for exiled religious leader Ayatollah Khomeini to come home – an act that hastened the political demise of his own government and strengthened the influence over events being exerted by the troops and the mullahs.

(previous page) Old barriers, new obstacles... Germans attack the Berlin Wall that divides them, 11 November 1989. (right) The Iran-Iraq War. State President Saddam Hussein addresses Iraqi forces shortly before the invasion of Iran, 25 September 1980. (above) Three years into the war, Donald Rumsfeld, an envoy of Secretary of State, George Schultz, shakes hands with Saddam Hussein, 20 December 1983.

The bitter war between Iran and Iraq was initially a battle for the oil-rich disputed province of Khuzistan. After four years of joint rule, Iraq's forces invaded the province in September 1980. The war ended eight years later, with a ceasefire negotiated by the United Nations. By that time more than a million combatants had been killed.

The immediate aftermath of the attempt by John F. Hinckley, Junior, to assassinate President Ronald Reagan outside the Hilton Hotel, Washington, DC, 30 March 1981.

The would-be assassin Hinckley fired five or six shots at the president, which wounded the president, his press secretary and a Secret Service agent. The incident brought out the showbiz best in ex-movie star Reagan, who joked with his wife that he had forgotten to duck, and with the surgeons who treated him that he hoped they were all Republicans. Hinckley was found 'not guilty' of attempted murder by reason of insanity.

Terrorist targets. (clockwise, from above) President Anwar Sadat of Egypt at a press conference, 13 February 1981. The assassination of Sadat by Islamic fundamentalists, Cairo, 6 October 1981. Pope John Paul II is held by aides after the attempt on his life by Mehmet Ali Agca, St Peter's, Rome, 13 May 1981.

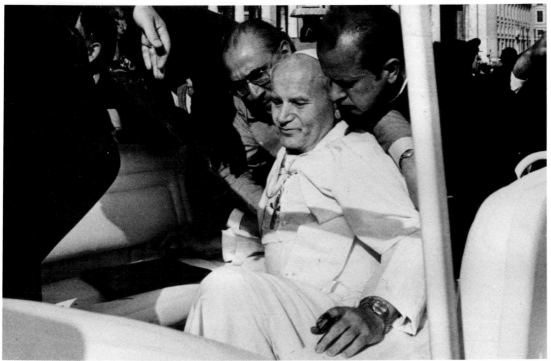

Sporting behaviour... (clockwise, from opposite, top) Björn Borg and John McEnroe, Wimbledon champions in 1980 and 1981, respectively. England football fans react after their country's 2–0 defeat by Switzerland in Basle, 1981. Ian Botham toils against the West Indies. Duncan Goodhew limbers up, 1980.

Punk and after... (above) Alice Cooper with a boa constrictor, *c*.1980. (right) Toyah Wilcox makes her own hair stand on end, *c*.1980.

(above) The Jamaican reggae star Bob Marley, a
few months before his death from cancer, 1980.
(left) 'I sing so that I can help someone overcome
a bad time' – Marvin Gaye, July 1980.

Royal distractions... (above) Queen Elizabeth II maintains control of her horse, Burmese, after the firing of six blanks by an unemployed 17-year-old during Trooping the Colour, 30 June 1981. (right) Prince Charles in control of proceedings at his marriage to Lady Diana Spencer, St Paul's Cathedral, London, 29 July 1981.

The Falklands War. (above) Argentinian bombs... The Royal Navy frigate HMS *Antelope* is blown apart in San Carlos Bay, 24 February 1982. (opposite) British bombs... Port Stanley's airport comes under heavy attack, 14 May 1982.

Extreme fashion statements of the 1980s... (opposite) Issey Miyaki's heavy-weight knitwear of 1982. (above) Two neo-punks in London's Hyde Park, 26 October 1986.

In the 1980s fashion dealt in the outrageous – in design, materials and presentation. Shows adopted the style of the pop video, and the line between fashion and showbiz became ever more blurred. The punk revival, meanwhile, had a commercial edge – some punks even charged to have their photographs taken in public.

The world's fashion icon in the 1980s – Diana, Princess of Wales... (above) at the premiere of *Back to the Future* and (opposite) leaving a Bruce Oldfield fashion show, both in 1985.

Arms drill... Frederick Bulsara (better known as Freddie Mercury) fronts the rock band Queen, 3 September 1984.

Madonna Louise Ciccone (better known simply as Madonna) at full stretch during the
Philadelphia Live Aid concert, 12 September 1985.

A Sudanese policeman holds back a crowd of starving refugees awaiting the arrival of a relief shipment of grain from the Save the Children Fund, 15 July 1985.

It was the summer of the 'global jukebox' with two Live Aid concerts in London and Philadelphia held simultaneously. The misery caused by drought, disease and civil war in Africa was brought to the attention of the world by television and press reports, and especially by the day-long concerts themselves, which were watched by more than 1.5 billion viewers worldwide and helped to raise millions in charitable donations.

СЛАВА ВОИНАМ-ИНТЕРНАЦИОНАЛИСТОМ!!!

Afghan warriors. (top) Mujahideen guerrillas help a wounded comrade in the Safed Koh mountains, 10 February 1988. (opposite, top) The body of an Afghan government soldier, killed in fighting near Jalalabad, 8 March 1989.

Soviet withdrawal. (opposite, bottom) Afghan officers salute departing Soviet troops (above), 15 May 1988. The departure followed an international agreement to end the foreign intervention in Afghanistan, which was signed by Afghanistan, the Soviet Union, Pakistan and the United States.

Bottoms up... (clockwise, from the top) Wimbledon players reveal their back formation, 16 May 1988. Florence 'Flo-Jo' Griffith-Joyner waits for her leg of the 4 x 100-metre sprint relay at the Seoul Olympics, September 1988. Boris Becker covers the court at the Paris Open, 1987.

Critic and worshippers... (opposite) Salman Rushdie with the new book that could have cost him his life, 11 February 1989 – three days later came the *fatwa*. (above) Mourners after the death of Ayatollah Ruhollah Khomeini, Tehran, 5 June 1989.

Death on the ground... (top) The burial of a child victim of the Union Carbide disaster at Bhopal, India, 3 December 1984. (opposite, top) The wall collapses at the Heysel Stadium, Brussels, 29 May 1985.

Death in the air... (above) The *Challenger* space shuttle explodes 74 seconds after take-off, 28 January 1986. (opposite, bottom) The wreckage of Pan Am Flight 103, Lockerbie, Scotland, 21 December 1988.

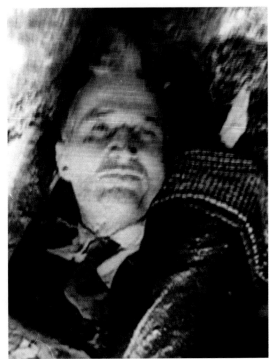

The old order dies... (left) Romanians gather outside the Communist Party Central Committee headquarters, Bucharest, 22 December 1989. One week later, their former dictator Nicolae Ceausescu (above) was executed.

President Reagan had labelled it the 'Evil Empire' and for forty years the Soviet Union held Eastern Europe in what seemed to be an iron grip. But the end when it came was swift. In December 1988, Soviet Premier Mikhail Gorbachev reduced the number of Soviet troops by 10 per cent, and within a year Poland, Hungary, East Germany, Czechoslovakia and Romania had rejected communism and broken free.

(previous page) An old conflict, a new hope. (above) President Clinton brings
Yitzhak Rabin (left) and Yasser Arafat (right) together at the White House,
13 September 1993. (above) A bird coated in oil from wrecked Kuwaiti oil
fields, 26 January. (opposite) Iraqi schoolchildren visit a Baghdad air-raid shelter on the 10th anniversary of its mistaken destruction by an Allied missile.

Refugees from war. Kurds in Bakhtara besiege a food convoy from the Safe Havens programme initiated by the United States, Britain and France, 18 April 1991.

Towards the end of Operation Desert Storm, President Bush's call to the Iraqi people to overthrow Saddam Hussein was answered with a rising of the Kurds in northern Iraq. The insurrection was brutally suppressed by Iraqi government troops, and hundreds of thousands of Kurds fled into the mountains along the border with Turkey. There they stayed, while the world wondered what should be done for them.

Four years after his release from prison, Nelson Mandela addresses an election rally in Ikageng Stadium, 31 January 1994. He was campaigning for the African National Congress (ANC) in South Africa's first non-racial, one-person-one-vote national election.

One hundred days after the Ikageng rally, Mandela, the former president of the ANC, became head of the government of South Africa. In his inauguration speech on 10 May he revealed the quest for racial harmony that had won him the Nobel Peace Prize in 1993: 'Never, never and never again shall it be that this beautiful land will experience the oppression of one by another... Let freedom reign. God bless Africa!'

Wasteland... the ruins of Grozny, March 1995.

In 1994, in the Caucasus, the republic of Chechnya under the leadership of President Dzhokhar Dudayev sought to break away from Russian control. The result was an invasion and a bitter war that lasted into the next century, which was a result of military incompetence and half-hearted engagement on the part of the Russians and stubborn resistance from the Chechen rebels.

Rivalling the dysfunctional
Simpsons as exemplars of the
woe and strife of family life...
(above) Bill Clinton at the height
of his budget impasse with the
US Congress. (opposite) Hilary
Clinton is wired for sound on
CNN's *Late Edition*, March 1995.
(right) Monica Lewinsky congratu-
lates Clinton on his re-election,
November 1996.

The new Russian dancing bear... President Yeltsin in party mood during an election rally in Rostov, near Moscow, 10 June 1996.

Boris Nikolayavich Yeltsin's rise to power in the Soviet Union was not easy. He was a protégé of Gorbachev and an advocate of perestroika. *However, in 1990 he was demoted from the politburo to a lowly administrative post when he clashed with conservatives. Only after the collapse of the USSR was he elected in 1991 to serve as President of the Russian Federation.*

A 'high-five' of rappers... (clockwise, from top left) Actor and rapper Ice-T; R. Kelly at the Rosemont Horizon, 1994; Sean 'P Diddy' Combs; Rapper Coolio; and Snoop Doggy Dog, 1997.

Stars in the wars. (clockwise, from opposite, top) Woody Allen (left) and Soon Yi Previn, January 1993; Winona Ryder is injured on her way into court, 3 June 2002; Hugh Grant and O.J. Simpson pose for the LAPD, in June 1995 and November 1998, respectively.

The charges against the celebrities covered a multitude of sins. Allen was accused by his former partner Mia Farrow of sexually abusing her adopted daughter, Dylan. Winona Ryder was arrested for shoplifting. Hugh Grant paid in more ways than one for his moment of 'divine' passion. Defending a double murder charge, Simpson's court appearances were more protracted – but he was acquitted by the jury.

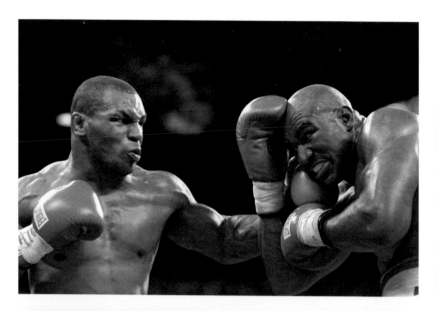

Red in tooth and claw... (top) Heavyweight Mike Tyson lands a blow on Evander Holyfield's jaw in their championship fight at the MGM Grand Garden Arena, Las Vegas, 28 June 1997. (above and opposite) Holyfield is in agony after Tyson had bitten off a piece of his right ear. Tyson was disqualified.

Just another day
on the West Bank...
A man (far right) is hit
by a rubber bullet as
Palestinians come
under fire from Israeli
troops in Hebron,
9 April 1997.

Wrecked homes, ruined lives. (top) A child plays war games in the remains of a house in Mostar, Bosnia-Herzegovina, 1 December 1994. (above) A young boy returns from a Kosovo refugee camp to a home that has been destroyed, October 1998.

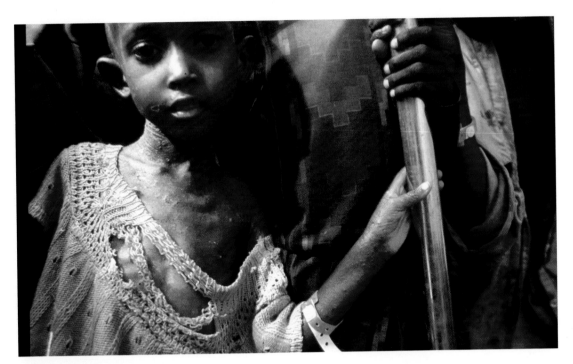

No homes, wrecked lives. (top) One of the thousands of young refugees from the civil war in Zaire, Kisangani, 15 April 1997. (above) Kosovar Albanians on their way to Bajram Curri in Albania during the Kosovar Albanian fight for independence from the Federal Republic of Yugoslavia, June 1998.

Genius laid bare... (clockwise, from opposite)
Damien Hirst prepares his work for Expo 1996 in
New York City; Rachel Whitehead's *Monument* – a
resin replica of the empty plinth in Trafalgar
Square, 2001; Jeff Koons's *Puppy* at New York
City's Rockefeller Center, June 2000.

*By the 1990s 'conceptual art' had gallery
walls and exhibition halls almost to itself.
Admirers saw brilliant and challenging
comment, beauty and even genius in the
works of Hirst, Yoshida, Emin, Creed,
Koons, Javacheff and many others.
Critics complained that there was often
'more sizzle than steak' in their creations.*

Designers stalk the catwalks... (clockwise, from opposite) Madonna steps out for Jean Paul Gautier; Alexander MacQueen presents his spring and summer Paris collection, 1998; John Galliano (centre) at the launch of Dior's perfume Addict, 2002; and Stella MacCartney acknowledges applause for her summer collection, Washington, DC, in 1999.

When worlds collide... (top) Islamic political activists demonstrate in Pakistan against cable television, 2000. (above) Bin Laden sympathisers protest in Quetta, Pakistan, 2001. (opposite) The apocalyptic image of the age – the World Trade Center at 9.03am on 11 September 2001. (following page) 13 September 2001

Women in the 21st century. (top) Preparing for a wedding in post-Taliban Afghanistan, Kabul, 29 August 2002. (above) Mother and son victims of the HIV-AIDS virus, Bouake, Ivory Coast, 13 July 2002.

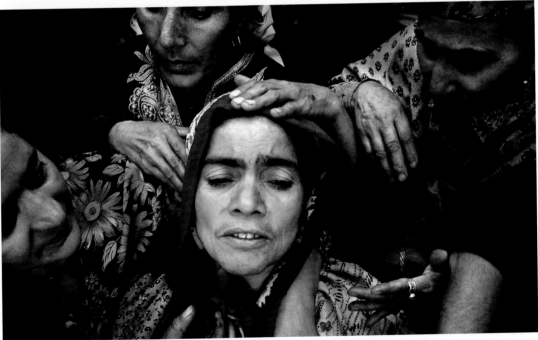

(top) Women who run a bakery in Bamiyan, Afghanistan, shelter from the wind, 27 June 2002.
(above) Mourners at the funeral of a woman killed in a political murder in Kashmir, 21 September 2002.

War on terrorism... (opposite) US troops take shelter during a battle with the Taliban near Mazar-i-Sharif, Afghanistan, 26 November 2001. (above) Some of the 160,000 Afghan refugees at a camp near Chaman, Pakistan, reach out for food supplies on 4 December 2001.

Going for gold. (clockwise, from top left) Ronaldo holds the World Cup, 30 June 2002; Serena Williams, 7 September 2002; Tiger Woods winning again, 22 September 2002; David Beckham scores against Argentina, 7 June 2002; Maria Mutola takes gold in the 100-metre sprint at Sydney, 2000.

(previous page) On the world stage... South Korean supporters at the FIFA World Cup quarter-final game against Spain in Gwangju, 22 June 2002. South Korea won 5-3 on penalties. (opposite) The threat of war, the price of peace... Saddam Hussein is sworn in as president of Iraq, 17 October 2002. (above) George W. Bush and Tony Blair present their timetables for diplomacy and war at a White House press conference, 31 January 2003. (left) US Secretary of State Colin Powell and German Foreign Minister Joschka Fischer (background) at odds with one another in Washington, DC, 30 October 2002.

(left) Coalition
intervention in Iraq
continues with missile
attacks on Baghdad, 21
March, 2003
(following page)
50,000 anti-war
protesters march from
the Brandenberg
Gate to the Victoria
Column in Berlin,
29 March, 2003.